Understanding Your
Child's Personality

DR. DAVID STOOP

Understanding Your Child's Personality

Discover your child's
unique personality type

Tyndale House Publishers, Inc.
WHEATON, ILLINOIS

Visit Tyndale's exciting Web site at www.tyndale.com

Published in association with the literary agency of Alive Communications, Inc., 1465 Kelly Johnson Blvd., Suite 320, Colorado Springs, CO 80920.

Designed by Brian Eterno.

Library of Congress Cataloging-in-Publication Data

Stoop, David A.
  Understanding your child's personality / David Stoop.
    p.   cm.
  ISBN 0-8423-7632-1 (hardcover : alk. paper)
  1. Typology (Psychology)   2. Myers-Briggs Type Indicator.
3. Personality in children.   4. Child rearing.   5. Parent and child.
I. Title.
BF723.P4S77   1998
155.4'1826—dc 21   97-32366

Printed in the United States of America

06   05   04   03   02   01   00   99   98
10   9   8   7   6   5   4   3   2   1

TABLE OF CONTENTS

"I Just Don't
Understand This Child!"

She was different, this cute little blonde twelve-year-old named Ashley. I have a granddaughter about the same age, and Ashley was certainly different from her. My granddaughter will talk and talk and talk about almost anything. But Ashley remained quiet and reserved through most of our conversation. However, when the subject turned to tennis, she came alive. "I'm going to play tennis professionally someday," she asserted with a newly revealed confidence. We had been talking about school, and her favorite descriptive word about school had been *boring*. But there was nothing boring about tennis to this young girl.

"How well do you play?" I asked.

"I've beaten my dad several times, and he thinks he's a pretty good player," she said. Then she tried to explain to me the way tennis players are rated. Now she was becoming quite animated. I asked her about any other sports she enjoyed. "Oh, I love soccer, but that's a team sport. I guess that's why I love tennis more—because it's all up to how well *I* play."

"Do you practice a lot?"

"Oh, they call it practice, but to me it's all fun. I just love to play!"

Ashley's father had asked me if I would see his daughter for one session. He was concerned that something might be wrong with her. "Maybe she has that attention-deficit thing—I don't know," he said to me, adding that several of her teachers had thought Ashley should be tested. "She has a real hard time staying interested in what the class is doing. Would you just talk to her a little? Maybe you can help me understand this child; I have never understood her. Ever since she started crawling I've wondered about her. But I don't want to attribute it all to some condition for fear she will be labeled—that is, unless it's really true."

We made the appointment. A week later Ashley was sitting across from me in my office.

Ashley was quiet, not just with me but apparently with most people. But all her quietness disappeared whenever she was on the soccer field, a tennis court, the playground at recess, or when she was talking to me about tennis. She was a natural athlete and thoroughly enjoyed playing almost any game. Whenever she played, you would never guess that this was the same quiet little girl who fidgeted and couldn't concentrate in class.

When we talked about school, Ashley sat back in her chair, her speech slowed down, and she lost a lot of her animation. "School is such a bore," she said. "I'll probably be a professional tennis player, so what difference does it make if I know all about the history of the California missions? All that stuff is just boring."

When I brought Ashley's father, John, into the room, I told him, "I don't think it's an attention problem. It may have more to do with personality. She's the type of child who loves action, which would explain her love for sports and her restlessness in the classroom. She's a natural at sports, so practicing is simply part of her play—it is part of the performance." I explained that Ashley's personality, which was a part of her when she was born, accounted for much of what he had not understood about her behavior.

"Who else in your or your wife's family is like Ashley?" I asked.

"Well, according to her mom, that should be easy to answer," replied John. "Marti has always said that Ashley is just like Marti's mom—Ashley's grandmother. I never paid much attention to that comparison, but from what you're saying, I can see that they really are a lot alike. It might help me understand Ashley better if I understood my mother-in-law better."

John was right. Even though each person God creates is uniquely different from any other, there are patterns of characteristics that can give us a frame of reference for understanding people better. It is in seeing and understanding these patterns that can help us better understand our kids and their personalities. For example, imagine the following scene.

It's free time on the playground. The schoolteachers have made several suggestions as to what the children could do, but the children have also been given the freedom to do what they want for half an hour. What would your child do in this situation? Although you might not know exactly what he or she would do, could you predict in some general way the type of activity your child would choose? Let's take a look at what happens with some children as they make their choices on that playground during the half hour of free time.

THE ORGANIZERS

One of the first children we meet is Brad. He's hard to miss, for he is right in the middle of a large group of children trying to get a game of kickball started. After all, that was one of the things the teachers had suggested they do, and Brad is up to the task of getting the game started. You can hear his voice above the other children's chatter, and soon he and a friend (whom we'll meet later) are choosing up sides before the game gets under way. While Brad has been negotiating with some of the other vocal children, Bill (whom we'll also meet later) and several others are quietly waiting for the "leaders" to make up their minds and get on with choosing the teams.

Brad's female counterpart is Margaret. She's over on the cement with a bunch of girls getting a game of hopscotch organized, another game suggested by one of the teachers. Margaret has enlisted several of the quieter ones, such as Miriam, to go and find some chalk so they can begin drawing the squares. Soon Margaret has everyone organized; the girls are lined up, and the game begins.

Both Brad and Margaret are "out there" children. They are quick to speak, often thinking as they talk. Their sense of order and need for closure make them junior administrators. Each took a suggestion from the teachers and organized a group of children to make it happen. They didn't start the game just because the teacher suggested it—they did it because it made sense to them and because they wanted to. Their young personalities have equipped them to already enjoy the task of getting everyone organized so the fun can begin.

THE MONITORS

Bill and Miriam are similar to Brad and Margaret, except that they are more quiet and "inside themselves." They want to play the game, and they could probably organize it as well. But the thought of organizing the game would only occur to them a little later on. They appear to be less aware of what is going on around them since they are more preoccupied with their own private worlds, but they are always monitoring their environment.

While Brad and Margaret are enthusiastically directing the other children to get organized for the game, Bill and Miriam are each clustered around two or three other friends, talking and patiently waiting. Even though they also have an internal sense of structure and like things to get started, you would only see these traits in Miriam or in Bill if there were no Brad or Margaret around to press ahead. If there were no Brad around, Bill might suddenly realize as he stands there talking with several friends that nothing is happening—no one is organizing the game. Only then would he take charge and organize the group. Both Bill and Miriam are quieter versions of Brad and Margaret.

Bill and Miriam could also be called the Cooperators. They cooperate with the teacher as well as with the other students. They can become easily frustrated with peers who are not as cooperative as they are, especially when it comes to cooperating with teachers or other authority figures. Whereas Brad and Margaret will organize the game because the job is there to be done and they want to play, Bill and Miriam might organize the game more out of a sense of duty—because the teacher said they should and because there is no one else present who can.

THE RELATORS

Now that the games of kickball and hopscotch are under way, we notice Julie in another part of the playground. She and a group of girls are sitting at the lunch tables talking a mile a minute. It seems that this group of girls is often together, and they love to talk. If you stand nearby and listen, you will notice that they often interrupt each other, and no one seems to mind. You will also notice that their conversation wanders all over the place, and no one seems to mind that either. By their enjoyment it appears that all that matters is that they are together and talking. A couple of girls who had tried to keep up with all the chatter eventually walk away. "I can't understand what they're talking about," one of them might say to herself or to her friend.

Sometimes Julie and her friends join in the games around the playground, but even then, their focus will be on friends and talking together. For them, the half hour on the playground will seem like only a few minutes—that's how much they quickly get lost in their conversations with each other.

Daren is very much like Julie. But because he is a boy, his friendliness will be more task oriented. He may be playing kickball with Brad's team, but he makes sure that he and most of his friends are on the same team. They are always chattering with each other on the field, and when they are on the bench, they seem to be having a party. Brad often has to interrupt Daren to let him know it's his turn at bat.

One of the fun things about Daren is that he usually has something he's willing to trade. It may be a pocketful of baseball cards, a baseball glove, or even one of the new puppies at home. Daren is a natural salesman, even on the playground. He'll make sure you want one of those puppies just because he's so excited about your having one of them.

Both Daren and Julie are curious about the world of ideas and about getting to know other people. Both of them are very enthusiastic about life, and they are usually very idealistic about their friendships.

THE DREAMERS

Jennifer is much like Julie, the Relator, except that she is more reserved. She has the same idealism and enthusiasm, but hers are more internal. Rather than sit and talk with a group of girlfriends, Jennifer can be seen walking around the perimeter of the playground with her one best friend—we'll call her Sally—deep in conversation. Sally is fairly new to the school. When Sally was introduced to Jennifer's class, she seemed uncomfortable and somewhat sad to be there. Jennifer felt her discomfort and immediately reached out to her. She invited Sally to have lunch with her, and their friendship resulted. Jennifer is always concerned about how others are feeling, especially those who are being treated unfairly by their peers or by a teacher. Sometimes Jennifer is so busy taking care of others that she barely has time to do the things she needs to do at home.

Dan is very much like Jennifer in that he is also more quiet and reserved than some of the other types. But rather than wander around the perimeter of the playground with a friend, he's sitting off by himself, watching what everyone else is doing. At least it appears that he is watching. But if we were to speak to him, we would probably find that he started out watching the others but ended up lost in a daydream. In his mind he's escaped to some exotic place in space or time. Perhaps he's fighting with the Indians they read about in class that morning. Or maybe he is thinking how he would have kicked in the winning run if he had chosen to play kickball. Dan's got several close friends who are interested in the same things he's interested in, but they are in a different class this year, and he sees them only after school.

What's interesting about both Jennifer and Dan is that they are very content with their small circle of friends. In their minds, there is a whole other world available through their imagination, and it seems senseless to crowd your life with too many people. Even though they are usually the only one or two in a classroom with this particular personality, they often find a kindred-spirit friend with whom they can relax and be themselves.

THE COMPETITORS

Calvin is the boy who chose up teams with Brad. While Brad organized the other kids who were going to play, Calvin was strategizing as to whom he would pick and whom he thought Brad would pick and whom he should pick first. Once the game starts, Brad has a great time playing kickball. But on the other side of the field, Calvin is much more intense with his team. To him the fun is in winning. So he is always trying to figure out what the opponents will be doing and then getting his team set up in some way that will neutralize the play. This intensity in Calvin is missing in Brad, but Calvin's intensity seems to limit the fun he could have at whatever he is doing. For Calvin, play is serious business, and whenever it is competitive, he is up to the challenge. Unfortunately, Calvin's seriousness doesn't always carry over into his classroom work.

Abbey is very much like Calvin. She is playing hopscotch and is very careful about how she plays—and she's determined to win. As the others take their turns, Abbey's strong sense of justice kicks in quickly if someone complains about a landing. Abbey can outargue any of them; she can even outargue most of the boys. Sometimes Abbey's logical abilities are a source of both joy and embarrassment to her. She doesn't mind being smarter than all the other girls, but there are times she does mind being smarter and more logical than most of the boys.

Abbey has to work hard at fitting in with the other girls. That's why she plays every game she can. If they hadn't played hopscotch, she would have been playing kickball. And she wouldn't have been the last one chosen, either. She is good at almost everything she tries, but she is never satisfied with her performance. To her, she could always have done better. Her self-criticism usually doesn't spill over onto others, but if it did, she would be sensitive enough to know it, stop, and make things right with the other person.

THE EXPLORERS

Carl is different from Calvin only in that he is quieter and more inner-directed. That little shift makes a big difference in how each of these boys lives his life. Rather than joining in with what the others are doing, Carl is usually off by himself, exploring. He has found an old piece of concrete and moved it, revealing a whole new world of bugs. For most of the time on the playground, Carl is lost in this bug world. He watches them scurry around to find the safety they lost when the rock was moved. He picks up one that he's never seen before and examines it carefully. He even has a magnifying glass in his pocket that helps him see what happens as he manipulates and dissects the bug by hand.

Annie is a lot like Carl. When she noticed that Carl was preoccupied off in a corner of the playground, she was curious and went to check on what was so interesting. At first, she couldn't have cared less about the bug population under the rock, but when Carl pulled out his magnifying glass, she was interested in seeing this strange new bug as well. When Carl pulled off a leg and tossed it at her, she simply gave him a disgusted look instead of the "typical" female reaction. As a result, they were soon having their own private science class, oblivious to the other kids on the playground. They were so engrossed in their microscopic world that they missed the bell signaling the end of the playground time. It took a teacher calling them by name to get them back into the classroom.

THE PLAYERS

Rick is always in motion. He often struggles just to stay in his seat in the classroom, so the playground is a welcomed break for him. He was ready to play kickball as soon as Brad started gathering the troops, but while Brad and Calvin were working out the details and choosing their teams, Rick had the ball and was already playing with a couple of friends. When Brad chose him on the second pick, he acknowledged it but went on kicking the ball back and forth with his two buddies. He is usually picked early, for he seems to be a natural athlete. He never practices much; he simply plays a lot—and he plays well.

All this organizational stuff is perfect for Brad, the Organizer, and even for Calvin, the Competitor, but not for Rick. It only serves to take time away from playing. In fact, if Rick had his way, everyone would just start playing and who cares how even the teams are! Rick is a player because he loves to play. All of life is a game to him, and it matters little who wins or loses, just so you get to play. After all, what's to live for if you can't get to play at least part of the time? Play is for play, not for any other purpose. One might say of children like Rick that they "major in recess."

Sandy loves to play also, but for her, playing is performing. She's often the center of attention because she is such a great entertainer. She loves an audience and knows how to keep them laughing. She joined in the hopscotch game not so much because she wanted to play the game but because that was where most of the girls were gathered. She's usually able to keep the boys laughing as well, but they were playing kickball, and they took their game too seriously for them to notice her entertaining them.

As the girls play hopscotch, Sandy is watching everyone and is quick to imitate anyone who does something unusual. If there's a lull in the action during the game, she may imitate the teacher that gets on everyone's nerves. There's always something to laugh about when kids are around Sandy. She's also the one who, during a tense time in a classroom, whispers some funny remark at just the right time to break the tension. Of course, she's often in trouble for what she says, but that's a small price to pay for being able to grab the spotlight and be on stage.

THE INDIVIDUALISTS

Ryan and Sarah are the quiet, inner-directed versions of Rick and Sandy, the Players. On the inside, they love fun and action just as much as Rick and Sandy do. They have a very different sense of humor, but that humor is an important part of their behavior.

Ryan joined Rick in playing on the sidelines while waiting for the teams to be chosen. But Ryan would have been content to stand by and wait for the game to begin, at least for a short time. His attention span is somewhat longer than Rick's, but he can only remain inactive so long.

Sarah is one of those who had left Jennifer's talkative group because she couldn't understand what the wandering conversation was all about. She had also left that group because just sitting around talking wasn't quite enough action for her. She likes to keep moving, but she can still concentrate as long as what she is focusing on is something tangible.

For example, Sarah has a real appreciation for color and texture. This is expressed in the clothes she chooses to wear. Not one to follow the crowd, Sarah will often dress in a way that is all her own. She may wear a hat to school or to the mall. Her sense of style can be seen in the splashes of color or variety of textures in her clothes. Her mom often can't quite understand her taste but has to admit, "It's Sarah!" Sarah is the epitome of the Individualists.

Both Ryan and Sarah are often misunderstood by their teachers, by their parents, and even by their peers. They seem, in many ways, to be like Jennifer and Dan, the Dreamers, in that they live in their own private world. But the active side of Ryan and Sarah, though not fully seen until late adolescence or adulthood, gives them a restlessness and an individualistic approach to life that is unique to their personality type. This restlessness is most often seen with school matters that somehow seem to them irrelevant to what life is really about. And, of course, in elementary school they really know what life's about—at least they think they do!

Did You See Your Child on the Playground?

Did we describe your child? If not, he or she may actually be one of the quieter types, which are harder to describe because most of what's going on is in their inner world.

As you begin to consider your child's personality traits, here are some questions you might consider:

- Why does my child choose certain activities over others?
- What has made my child the way she or he is?
- How can I better understand the whys behind my child's actions?

In the pages ahead, we're going to help you better understand your child's personality. In doing so, we'll address some specific questions:

Chapter 2
What is "normal" for personality?
What are the basic personality types?
What is my personality type?

Chapter 3
When and how will I begin to recognize my child's personality type?
What traits does my child prefer, and what does that say about him or her?
Is my child Extraverted or Introverted, Sensing or iNtuitive, Thinking or Feeling, Judging or Perceiving?

Chapter 4
Out of the sixteen possible combinations of personality traits, how do we arrive at the four basic personality types?
What are the four basic personality types, also called temperaments, and what are their main characteristics?

Chapters 5–8
Based upon my child's temperament:

- What captures her attention?
- How does he handle school? tasks? family and holidays? discipline? responsibility? relationships?

- What are sources of stress to my child?
- What special parenting tasks are required to handle a child with this temperament?

How does an Introverted child with this temperament compare to an Extraverted child with this same temperament?

Chapter 9
What kinds of mistakes might I make if I don't understand my child's personality?
How can I encourage my child to be who God made her to be?
How can I help my child develop his strengths and not be discouraged by his weaknesses?
How can I help my child, regardless of her temperament, to develop a healthy emotional life?

Chapter 10
What might cause serious personality clashes between me and my child?
What can I do if my child's personality style drives me crazy?

Chapter 11
How does my child's temperament affect the way she approaches her spiritual life?
What specific things can I do to help my child develop spiritually according to the personality God has given him?

Chapter 12
Eleven questions most frequently asked by parents.

Understanding Your Child Better

This first chapter gave an overview of basic personality types among children. In the following chapters we will introduce other terms describing personality. But at this point, be aware that the eight personalities met so far can be categorized into two basic areas: outward-directed, or extraverted, personalities and inward-directed, or introverted, personalities. These eight types are divided accordingly:

EXTRAVERTS	INTROVERTS
___Organizers	___Monitors
___Relators	___Dreamers
___Competitors	___Explorers
___Players	___Individualists

To get started on your evaluation of your own child or children, check the personality type you think your child has, based upon the information you have so far.

CHAPTER TWO

"You Mean You Can Describe Personality?"

Remember back to when your child was a tiny newborn. As he or she lay there quietly in your arms (or perhaps fussed and cried because of colic), the personality of your child lay undeveloped. You could say that your child's personality was, at that time, waiting to emerge. Gradually, around the third to fifth month, that tiny little boy's or girl's personality began to develop.

It's an incredible experience to see how that tiny baby's physical makeup is wonderfully "knit together" by God. The little hands and feet are part of God's beautiful handiwork. Then, when we think of what is inside that infant—a heart, a stomach, lungs, intestines, a complex brain that will eventually control every aspect of the child's mind and body—we are even more amazed.

We should be equally in awe of the complexity of a baby's personality. It is something that makes every human different from every other human. Yet when God makes something, there is within it a simplicity that makes it understandable to us. Within our multifaceted personality exists a simplicity that helps us understand this remarkable part of creation.

But how does personality develop? What are some "benchmarks," or standards, by which one could evaluate personality? After all, we know the "normal" range of children's height or weight at any given point in their growth. We know what intellectual abilities they should have at one year, give or take a couple of months. We can even identify what social skills children should possess at age three or when they begin kindergarten. We have these "norms" for the physical development of children and for their intellectual and social development. But what do we know about personality development?

WHAT IS NORMAL?

Because so little has been written to help parents understand their child's personality, they will sometimes wonder if their child is "normal." What parents don't realize is that their own perception of normal is based upon their own personality! We think our child is developing normally if we can recognize in his or her personality some traits that are similar to ours. But if those traits are different from ours, we have no frame of reference to tell us what is acceptable.

Some parents might watch their child on the playground doing very typical things for the child's particular personality type, but because the child is different from them, his or her behavior becomes cause for concern.

For example, Sarah, one of the Individualists we met on the playground, has a mother who is very conservative in her mannerisms and is also very outgoing in nature. Sarah's "wild clothing," as her mother calls it, causes Sarah's mother concern. She is convinced that Sarah is being rebellious and irresponsible in the way she dresses. She talks often with other mothers about her embarrassment at some of the outlandish ways Sarah puts clothes together. She is also concerned that Sarah is too much of a loner and that something is wrong—perhaps she has destroyed Sarah's self-esteem with her earlier criticism of Sarah's choice of dress.

What Sarah's mother doesn't understand is that she and her daughter may be looking at the same thing, but their *perception* of what they are looking at will be completely different. For example, Sarah's mother looks at clothes in a very utilitarian way. She thinks you wear clothes to cover your body and to keep you warm. Clothing should be practical, useful, and reasonably attractive. On the other hand, Sarah looks at clothing as a statement about herself. Sarah is quiet, but she lets her clothing speak on her behalf. She likes loud colors and unusual patterns and combinations. Her clothes state, "I may be quiet, but I'm here!"

If Sarah's mother is concerned about her daughter's weight, height, or physical development as she grows, she can ask Sarah's pediatrician. If she is concerned about Sarah's academic or social development, she can ask Sarah's teachers. But whom can Mom ask about those "quirky" personality traits that just don't make sense to her?

THE BIRTH OF A PERSONALITY TYPE

When Sarah was born, she had within her an innate personality type that was inherited from the gene pool of both her parents' families. This personality isn't seen in the beginning, but as she grows and develops, her innate personality begins to show itself. (This process will be discussed in chapter 3.) Some of her traits are like her mother's and some are like her father's. Some may even be like a grandparent's or an aunt's or uncle's. But how can we identify these traits? Unless we have some theoretical base to draw from, we can't really understand how these traits work together to form Sarah's uniqueness.

Building on the personality theory of C. G. Jung, a Swiss psychiatrist who died in 1961, two women, Katherine Briggs and her daughter, Isabel Briggs Myers, expanded Jung's theory and developed the *Myers-Briggs Type Indicator®*. This is a scientifically validated self-reporting questionnaire that is used to increase self-understanding of our personality as well as to better understand those we love. (Recently, the Murphy-Meisgeier Type Indicator for Children was developed to help parents and teachers better understand the personalities and learning styles of children ages six to sixteen.[1] If interested, you might have a professional administer this test to your child.)

According to Myers-Briggs, each of us is born with a predisposition toward certain personality traits. They suggest that there are four pairs of opposite traits. You are either

Extraverted (E)	or	**I**ntroverted (I)
Sensing (S)	or	i**N**tuitive (N)
Thinking (T)	or	**F**eeling (F)
Judging (J)	or	**P**erceiving (P)

We all have a natural bent toward one trait in each pair, which will lead to our having four personality traits that we favor. For example, Sarah probably favors the characteristics

[1] For more information on both the *Myers-Briggs Type Indicator* and the Murphy-Meisgeier Type Indicator for Children, contact Consulting Psychologists Press, Inc., 3803 Bayshore Road, Palo Alto, CA 94303.

of Introversion, Sensing, Feeling, and Perceiving (more on each of these later). Her personality type would be one of the sixteen possible combinations of these eight traits. No trait is better or worse than any other. They are simply different.

As we describe Sarah's and her mother's preferences or natural bents, we could just as easily be saying that Sarah is left-handed and her mother is right-handed. Think of how each of them would favor one hand over the other. They each have two hands, but Sarah's mother, being right-handed, will favor her right hand over her left hand. She will use her right hand more often, and consequently over time, she will develop its abilities more clearly. In the same way, Sarah will prefer to use and develop her left hand. That doesn't mean either of them cannot use the other hand—they can. They just know which hand they prefer to use.

Sarah's preference for introversion makes her different from her mother, who prefers extraversion. Sarah is capable of extraverted behavior, just as her mother is capable of introverted behavior. But these are not their preferences— the behaviors they lean toward naturally. Beginning early in our growth and development as a person, we each have this natural predisposition to choose and develop one prefer- ence over its opposite. What we choose early in life will stay with us throughout our life. Our basic preferences really don't change, although with time and years, we can become more comfortable with the opposite of our initial prefer- ences. Sometimes, during certain stages of life, we may be forced to adapt our behavior as circumstances require, but even then, our core preferences will remain intact, if not so visible. While sometimes a serious trauma will bring about changes in a person's personality, most people do not expe- rience fundamental personality change.

To better understand each of the preferences, let's look

more carefully at each pair of traits. As we do this here in chapter 2, we will describe the traits as they apply to an adult, so think first in terms of yourself. We'll look at these traits in reference to your children in the following chapters. Our ability to understand our child's personality will be successful only to the degree that we are able to understand our own personality.

EXTRAVERSION VS. INTROVERSION: WHICH WORLD DO YOU RELATE TO?

Some people relate more to the world outside themselves—people and environment. Others relate more to the world within themselves—ideas and imagination.

Traits of an Extravert

If you are an Extravert, you relate primarily to an external world and draw energy from your interactions with those in your external world. You tend to think out loud because getting your thoughts out and into the external world helps you deal with them. It's almost as if the thought enters your brain, and before you know it, it has already slipped out of your mouth. People and activity can easily distract you. You enjoy talking with a group of people and will often be the one introducing others who are joining the group. Going to a party where you don't know everyone may not always be comfortable for you, but it is a challenge, and you will soon be energized by your efforts to get to know the other people.

If you are an Extravert, you are willing to try new things, like, for example, the new game announced at the party. You find that you can best understand something new by experiencing it. When you go home from the party, you often feel energized by your interactions with all the people

you talked to there. You need and enjoy affirmations from
other people about who you are or how well you do something. You need this kind of feedback from others. Sometimes you may feel shy, but your real preference and desire
is to be involved with other people. You are an expressive
person and enjoy a large number of friends. When you are
tired, spending some time with good friends can recharge
your batteries. However, when you get burned out, you
want to withdraw completely from your external world.
When you do this, you often sleep for twelve hours, and
then you're ready to go again.

▶▶ **For an Extravert, some of the fun of an event is being
able to talk about it afterward. Sometimes it's hard to
feel that you have really experienced the event until
you are able to talk about it.**

Traits of an Introvert
If you are an Introvert, you relate primarily to an internal
world, and you draw energy by getting away from the
external world so that you can focus internally. Talking
with a group of people can be very draining; you much
prefer to talk with one person at a time. In fact, if you go
to a party where you don't know everyone, you will find
someone who is interested in the things you are and
spend the evening talking with that person. You aren't
comfortable trying out a new game at the party, much
preferring to escape to the bathroom in the hope that the
others will start without you. That way you can watch and
see whether or not you might enjoy the game before having to join in. You want to understand something *before*
you experience it.

When you finally go home after the party, you will be drained of energy by all the interaction, even if you talked with only one person. You don't need as many friends as the Extravert does, and you tend to have long-term friendships with just a few people. You are very reflective and appear to others to be mysterious or reserved. You tend to process things in your mind before saying them. You are able to concentrate, sometimes even to the point of shutting out external distractions completely. When you are tired, you need to recharge your batteries alone or perhaps with someone who will respect your need to withdraw into yourself.

▶▶ **A mother who is the only Introvert in her family of six has always tried to have a place where she could be alone. But anytime someone found her trying to enjoy her "aloneness," that person would shout, "Hey, everybody, come on; Mom's here alone and she needs some company!" Needless to say, Mom didn't agree, nor did she want or need the company.**

In our culture, there are three Extraverts to every Introvert. As a result, even Introverts can be led to believe that it is better to be an Extravert. This isn't true at all. There are no good or bad types. In fact, both types of traits are perfectly normal. It is when we are able to accept ourselves as God made us that we can develop good mental, emotional, and spiritual health.

Understanding Your Child Better

As you think about yourself, decide whether you are an Extravert or an Introvert. Remember, you have some of both traits, but one will be more dominant. It will be your *preferred* way of relating or acting. If you have difficulty deciding, ask the opinion of someone who knows you. Or look back over the descriptions and ask yourself which trait requires more effort from you. Extraverts can learn how to do Introverted things, but it is an effort for them. The same is true of Introverts; they can learn how to do Extraverted things, but it will always be an effort. The one that requires more effort is *not* your preference. Check which trait is your preference.

___Extraversion (E)   or   ___Introversion (I)

Now take a moment or two and think back to when you were a child and reflect on the following questions:

- Can you think of some situations or experiences that typify your preference for extraversion or introversion?
- How did your family affirm your being either an Extravert or an Introvert? How did they not accept this preference in you?
- Can you think of times when being either an Extravert or an Introvert caused you difficulty with others or led to your being misunderstood?

SENSING VS. INTUITION: HOW DO YOU TAKE IN INFORMATION?

Some people take in information through their five senses and leave it at that. Others use those senses but seem to operate more from their "sixth" sense.

Traits of a Sensing person

If you are a Sensing person, you tend to take in information around you through your senses. If you can see it, taste it, touch it, hear it, or smell it, then it exists for you. As a result, you are a very concrete, literal person. Common sense and "earthy wisdom" are your strengths. *Practical, realistic,* and *sensible* are words that are music to your ears. You are oriented to the here and now, and because of this you are very interested in results that can be seen quickly. If you are pushed too far into the future, it can appear frightening or bleak.

You tend to do things in a linear pattern, working step-by-step. This means you also enjoy the details and are much more interested in facts and figures than in ideas or brainstorms. When you look at a forest, all you can see are the individual trees. Consequently, you often miss the big picture. So you take these facts and figures in a very literal way. In school you liked true/false tests or ones where you had to fill in the blanks with specific answers. Your literal approach to things means you may not be too interested in interpreting what they mean. This can be a problem when talking with an iNtuitive person, for you are not sure whether to take him literally. You may have to ask, "Are you serious or just kidding?" You work hard and wish everyone else did as well. You have a very down-to-earth approach to problems and people.

▶▶ **Most accountants are Sensing. Can you imagine giving the IRS a "best-guess" at a deduction? Most Sensing accountants can even remember what was on line 17B of a 1040 form from last year!**

Traits of an iNtuitive person
If you are an iNtuitive person, you tend to take in information around you through your intuition. (We highlight the

letter *N* because we have already used the letter *I* for
Introversion.) Reality exists in the world of ideas and
possibilities. In school, you liked the essay tests best, for
you could express a lot of what you knew about a subject
and in that essay *somewhere* give the right answer. You
tend to answer questions by giving more information
than might have been requested. Following specified
steps to arrive at a goal is frustrating, even boring, to you.
You'd rather just somehow "get there." As a result, you
find that often you have overlooked an important detail
that would have helped you in the process. You tend to
be an inferential communicator; you often say less than
what you mean but assume the listener can fill in the rest.

▶▶   **A Sensing person and an iNtuitive person were in a**
strange city to meet with a professor and got lost.
The Sensing person wanted to call for directions,
knowing it would save time. But the iNtuitive person
said, "No, we can figure it out. The professor we are
meeting does research at the hospital; the hospital
must be near the university, which is back by the
stadium we just went past. I think we can find it."

Facts and figures may be important to you but only in
terms of how they fit into the bigger picture. You seldom see
the individual trees, because you are in awe of the forest. You
tend to think globally, becoming bored with step-by-step
instructions. For you, the adage that if it isn't broken, don't fix
it is nonsense; things can always be improved. And anyway,
you just might want to take it apart to find out how it works.
Looking only at the now feels stuck—you much prefer to live
in the future. In fact, in many ways today is only a stepping-
stone to what is really important—tomorrow. You probably

don't balance your checkbook too often, for you just have an intuitive feel for how much is in your account.

Imagination is far more enjoyable than reality, even to the point where anticipating a trip can be more fun than actually taking the trip. You enjoy metaphors or analogies as well as puns and word games.

Understanding Your Child Better

Which is your preference—sensing or intuition? Remember that you will have some of both traits, but one will be more dominant or will be your preferred way of operating. There are also times when a Sensing person wants to sit and daydream like the iNtuitive person, just as there are times of urgency when the iNtuitive person has to be precise like the Sensing person. And remember the way to decide if you can't figure out your choice: Ask a friend who knows you, or look at what you have to work harder at doing. If you have to work harder at the Sensing skills, you are an iNtuitive; if you work hardest at the iNtuitive skills, you are Sensing.

In our culture, there are three Sensing people for every iNtuitive person, so our culture will value the Sensing traits and put pressure on us to be that way. For the iNtuitive person, life has often felt like an experience of "swimming upstream." Check which trait is your preference.

___Sensing (S)   or   ___iNtuitive (N)

Now take a moment or two and think back to when you were a child and reflect on the following questions:

- Can you think of some situations or experiences that typify your preference for sensing or intuition?

- How did your family affirm your being either a Sensing or an iNtuitive person? How did they not accept this preference in you?
- Can you think of times when being either Sensing or iNtuitive caused you difficulty with others or led to communication problems?

THINKING VS. FEELING: HOW DO YOU MAKE DECISIONS?

Some people work out problems with logic, data, and a clear sense of the "right way to do it." Other people figure in the feelings of others and their own value systems much more than they do logical arguments.

Traits of a Thinking person

If you are a Thinking person, you make decisions with your head. You are an objective, coolheaded person who enjoys making a pros-and-cons list before deciding. You are more firm than gentle in a discussion, sometimes needing to be reminded to be tactful. In a disagreement, it is often more important to you that the issue be discussed and analyzed thoroughly than to have everyone arrive at agreement on the issue. As a result, others sometimes see you as being cold, perhaps even going so far as to say you have "ice in your veins."

The truth is, you do have feelings; you just don't talk about them very often. If forced to choose, justice is a more important virtue than mercy. You tend to analyze a problem over and over again until you understand it. When you discuss your views on some issue, you have your arguments numbered and ordered in a very logical way. If they are not numbered literally, you may use your fingers to "tick off" each point. If someone asks you "How do you feel about . . .?" you will usually respond by saying, "I think that. . . ." You sometimes like to play "devil's advocate" just to keep your mind sharp. In the same way, you can often argue both sides of an issue with equal clarity and enthusiasm.

▶▶ **A Thinking man said, "I have feelings; it's just that they seem big and dumb and dangerous, like the Incredible Hulk."**

Traits of a Feeling person

If you are a Feeling person, you make decisions with your heart. You are a subjective person who considers a decision to be good if everyone's feelings have been taken into consideration. You are more gentle than firm and will often give in during a disagreement because you want to keep things pleasant. You find it easy to understand what someone else is feeling in any given situation, and you are able to make decisions that take these feelings into consideration. A pros-and-cons list, which is an objective decision-making tool, leads to a bad decision for you. You make good decisions when you listen to that inner voice of your heart, even though you cannot always give reasons for your decision.

You become uncomfortable in a long discussion that is obviously not going to be unanimous in its outcome. In fact, you usually find that you are embarrassed by conflicts, even though you are not involved in the outcome. You have a tendency to personalize things that aren't meant to be personal. If forced to choose, mercy is valued more than justice, for it takes into consideration the extenuating circumstances. If you ask a Feeling person, "What do you think about . . .?" he or she will inevitably respond by answering, "Well, I feel that. . . ."

▶▶ **A Thinking husband said about his Feeling wife, "Feeling people don't want only agreement from you, they want conversion."**

Understanding Your Child Better

In our culture about half the population are Thinkers and half are Feelers. But gender plays a role in this pair of traits, and only in this pair. About two-thirds of men are Thinkers, and about two-thirds of women are Feelers. You can see that this distribution probably has something to do with sex-role stereotypes, which say that men are analytical and women are sentimental. Again, neither trait is good or bad, and it is neither good nor bad if a man is a Feeler or if a woman is a Thinker. If you fall into this category, there may be times when you've felt you haven't "fit in" because your preference went against the stereotype, but it is not a question of good or bad. Decide which is your preference and mark it below.

___Thinker (T)   or   ___Feeler (F)

Now take a moment or two and think back to when you were a child and reflect on the following questions:

- Can you think of some situations or experiences that typify your preference for thinking or feeling?
- How did your family affirm your being either a Thinking or a Feeling person? How did they not accept this preference in you?
- Can you think of times when being either a Thinker or a Feeler caused you difficulty with others?
- Can you think of times when you didn't use your preference and you made a bad decision?

JUDGING VS. PERCEIVING: HOW DO YOU ORGANIZE YOUR EXTERNAL WORLD?

Some people are well organized and decisive. Others prefer an open-ended world in which all the information is never quite in.

Traits of a Judging person

If you are a Judging person, it does not mean you are judgmental—although you may have been called that. It does mean that you are comfortable making judgments and decisions. You are a decisive person, thinking that it is better to make a bad decision than no decision at all, for at least the matter is decided. If it is a wrong decision, you can deal with that later. Structure, organization, order, and planning ahead are important values to you. You like to plan your work and then work your plan. If you have a big project, you want to break it down into smaller pieces, define what steps need to be taken, and then list the order in which you are going to do things. For you, a deadline is when you are to be finished, so you begin work early so that you are often finished even before the deadline. You are good at time management and are more than willing to help others learn how to manage their time better.

Closure is one of your favorite words. You are always most comfortable when the job is finished. In fact, it is hard for you to stop in the middle of a job and play. You can't really enjoy the play until the job is finished. As a parent, you not only teach your children to finish something before starting something else, you model it for them. The joy of any task is in the finished product. You have a public sense of organization. Your files are open to others. And even though you are not always perfectly organized, your strength is in maintaining your organization. Planning things ahead gives you a sense of security. You don't like last-minute changes in plans or unexpected things to crop up in your day.

▶▶ **A software consultant said that whenever he is showing a Judging person how to work a program, he always uses meaningless data in his demonstrations. "If I let them use data that's important to them, they get so interested in a finished product that they never pay attention to the process I'm trying to teach them."**

Traits of a Perceiving person
If you are a Perceiving person, it means that you are more comfortable at gathering information in order to make a decision than you are at actually making a decision. In fact, you will put off a decision until the last possible moment, just in case additional information comes along that might influence your decision. To make a bad decision is ridiculous. You prefer to put off the decision and gather more information. In fact, if you are forced to make an early decision, you are very uncomfortable. But if you have a big project to work on, you will take some time to look at what needs to be done and then just jump in and get started. You'll figure out what you need as you go along.

Flexibility, spontaneity, adaptability —these are the words that best describe you. You are comfortable juggling a number of tasks at one time, seeming to have the unique ability to get something done just when it needs to be done. For you, a deadline is often the starting bell. But you work quickly and stay up all night so that the task is finished on time. Whereas the Judging person would be flustered by too many tasks at one time, you flourish in that environment. *Open-ended* is your favorite term because it describes your wait-and-see attitude about life. You have a play ethic that allows you to stop working at any time and thoroughly enjoy playing.

As a parent, you try to teach your children to be Judging in their actions, such as putting things away before starting something new, but you do not model this for them, since you probably have at least five things started all at the same time.

Your organization is private. Rather than files, you organize in piles. And if anyone moves your piles, you can't find anything. You are always organizing, never quite getting to the place where it is finished. If you ever do finish, it is a struggle to keep it organized. You don't like to plan things too decisively, for it feels as if you are being pinned down. Keeping your options open is very important to you.

▶▶ **A Perceiving son said to his Judging father, "I think it would be totally depressing to know what I'm going to do all day."**

This pair of traits can be the source of a lot of frustration in relationships and within families. Children, especially teenagers, seem to all go through a stage of being disorganized. That doesn't mean they are all Perceiving people, only that they are in a messy and somewhat rebellious stage in life, although the Perceiving teenager will probably carry some degree of messiness throughout life.

Understanding Your Child Better

In our culture, about 55 percent of the population are Judging and 45 percent are Perceiving. As a result of that slight majority, schools, corporations, and even families tend to place a higher value on the Judging preference. Perceiving people often struggle with their natural bent, believing it is somehow wrong to be that way. But once again, each trait has its strengths and weaknesses, and neither is good or bad. It's just the way God made each of us. As you look at yourself, decide which is your preference.

   ___**J**udging (J)   or   ___**P**erceiving (P)

Now take a moment or two and think back to when you were a child and reflect on the following questions:

- Can you think of some situations or experiences that typify your preference for judging or perceiving?
- How did your family affirm your being either a Judging or a Perceiving person? How did they not accept this preference in you?
- Can you think of times when being either Judging or Perceiving caused you difficulty with others or led to your being misunderstood?

Look at how each pair of traits fits on the chart below:

Where do I focus my attention?

EXTRAVERT (E)	INTROVERT (I)
My primary focus is on the external world.	My primary focus is on the internal world.

How do I take in information?

SENSING (S)	INTUITIVE (N)
I use my five senses to take in information about the world.	I use my sixth sense—intuition—to take in information about the world.

How do I make decisions?

THINKING (T)	FEELING (F)
I make my best decisions by using my logic and analytic skills.	I make my best decisions by using my personal values and sentiments.

How do I organize my external world?

JUDGING (J)	PERCEIVING (P)
I like things orderly and planned in advance.	I like to be flexible and enjoy being spontaneous.

Now look back at each of the four pair of traits and write below what your preference in each was.

E or I   S or N   T or F   J or P

_____   _____   _____   _____

This will be our starting point. It doesn't mean that you now understand yourself. It does mean, though, that you have a foundation for understanding yourself, which is a prerequisite to understanding your child's personality. You'll see as we go along that, based on the four letters that describe you, you will be able to identify four basic temperaments. These four temperaments, each subdivided into introversion or extraversion, are represented by the eight types of children we met on the playground in chapter 1. Now that you have the four letters that describe you, let's look more closely at how these preferences appear in our children.

CHAPTER THREE

"What about My Child's Personality?"

What we described in the last chapter about your personality is going to be true in your child as well. She will have a preference for four of the traits, and her preference will shape her personality. But since these preferences are developed over time, it will not be as easy to see each of these preferences in a child at any given time. These personality traits seem to develop in an orderly way as the child grows.

How a Child's Personality Develops

The first personality trait that reveals itself in a child is the preference for either extraversion or introversion. We can observe this early in an infant's life by noticing her reaction to other people and new situations. The reserve of the Introvert will be seen as a hesitation in approaching the unfamiliar. The Extravert will be open to other people and to new situations around her.

The infant who clings to Mom when guests come to the house is probably an Introvert, whereas the child who is curious about the visitor and willing to look at the guest and respond to the guest's baby talk is probably going to be an Extravert. The toddler who holds your eyes with her eyes and then gives you a shy smile is probably a budding Extravert. The one who doesn't even notice you looking at her is an Introvert. The preschool kids in the van in front of you who are waving at you and everyone else who passes them are all Extraverts. The Introvert isn't even looking out the window, or if she is, she is not waving; she is looking at people only to try to figure out why the other kids are enjoying waving at you so much.

We might begin to see a preference for either judging or perceiving when a child is eighteen to twenty-four months old. Sometimes this preference will become obvious by age two, showing itself in the way the child wants her room organized, how well she will keep things organized, and how comfortable she is in stopping one activity in order to do something else. If we don't see this by age two, it doesn't mean that there's a problem in the child's development. It may mean that she is the Perceiving type who is open to a number of ways of doing things, including the way she organizes.

Usually we have a pretty good understanding of a child's personality preferences for either sensing or intuition and thinking or feeling by the time she begins school. These preferences will continue to develop into the child's adolescent stage and during that time will become even more easily identified. But we can begin to see the emerging of the preferences between sensing vs. intuition and between thinking vs. feeling, usually through a child's behavior, somewhere around preschool age.

We must keep in mind that the purpose of understanding our child's personality is not to label or to limit her. We study her personality so that we can affirm her strengths and encourage her full development as a person. Counselors have discovered over the years that parents are better able to accept a child's traits when there is some explanation for them and when those traits can be seen as normal for the child, even if those traits are not shared by other family members. This is a primary goal of this book—to help you as a parent understand your child and accept her traits, even those that are different from yours.

Now let's look at how each of these preferences develops in our children.

THE EXTRAVERTED CHILD

This child is more comfortable relating to the external world.

She is comfortable with new places, people, and events. If your child prefers extraversion, she will relate comfortably with the external world. New people, places, and events are welcomed by the Extravert. She likes to talk to you, and when she is young, she may talk out loud to you even when you are not there. When placed in a new environment, she may at first hesitate, but usually she is the first to say hi and join in with the rest of the group with relative ease. My granddaughter, an Extravert, could not wait for kindergarten to begin. Her first day was even more exciting than she had anticipated, and it couldn't have come soon enough. She had four new friends on the first day and left the classroom hand in hand with her teacher. Like other Extraverted children, she reveals a lot about herself soon after meeting you, because she has no hesitation in talking to you.

She talks as she learns. In the classroom, Extraverted

children are generally the ones with their hands up first. Sometimes when the teacher calls on an Extravert, she begins at that point to formulate out loud her response to the question. She hasn't thought through the answer; she simply knows she can come up with the answer and will formulate it as she talks. An Extraverted child tends to "think out loud." It's important for parents to remember that what the Extraverted child says out loud is not her final viewpoint on an issue. Like the Extraverted adult who wishes she could take back what she said too quickly, so will the Extraverted child wish that—if a parent takes everything the child utters as the bottom line. A wise teacher will allow Extraverted children to whisper to each other as a new concept is being introduced to the class. The soft "buzzing" sound in the classroom simply means that the Extraverted children are talking softly, either to a neighbor or to themselves, about what they are learning.

She doesn't like solitude. This type of child is full of energy when she is around other people, which is her preferred way of living. Solitude is not something the Extraverted child can tolerate. If there is no one else to play with, she will be constantly asking, "What can I do?" Even though she can be easily distracted when there is a lot going on, it is almost impossible to distract her from her own feeling of boredom when forced to entertain herself.

She needs affirmation—cues from the external environment. An Extravert's dependence on the external environment means that she likes a lot of affirmation. She seeks feedback from others about her ideas and behaviors. If she cleaned the kitchen, she wants to know that you noticed and that you appreciate what she did.

This dependence on the external world can be interpreted, especially by an Introverted parent, as the child's failure to learn how to rely upon herself. She may actually be very self-reliant, but she needs to know how she is being perceived by others in her external world.

She is easily distracted. An Extraverted child has a more difficult time with distractions. If she sits by a doorway or window and can see what is going on in the hallway or on the playground, she will have a hard time paying attention in the classroom. The same is true when she has to concentrate on doing her homework. Siblings playing nearby or a TV on in the background can distract the Extravert all too easily when what she is working on requires concentration. But she is able to watch TV and review her spelling list at the same time, for reviewing homework doesn't require too much concentration. When it is time to watch TV, the Extraverted child will usually want someone (or everyone else in the family) to watch TV with her.

THE INTROVERTED CHILD

This child is more comfortable relating to the inner world.

He must understand an environment before being comfortable in it. If your child is an Introvert, he will not be as comfortable relating to the external world. The first day of school can be very frightening, even intimidating. He wants Mom to stay so he will at least know someone. By the second or third day of school he has come to understand the environment, and his fear of the new has subsided; an Introvert needs to understand a situation, location, or process before he can experience it comfortably.

He processes internally before verbalizing. Every Introverted child struggles to be able to do things at his own pace. For example, he seldom raises his hand when the teacher asks a question because the teacher has already called on the Extravert who raised her hand immediately. The Introverted child is going to think through the answer and then raise his hand—not before. When he does answer, it is usually short and to the point. An Introvert will, of course, talk more freely with family and friends, but even then, his speech will be slower and more deliberate than an Extravert's speech.

He needs solitude and downtime. When an Introvert comes home from school, he needs some quiet downtime. He is not going to volunteer how his day went, and he doesn't want you to ask right away. He may be drained by all his interacting with others at school and need some time alone to get his batteries recharged. For example, Geoff would frequently come home from kindergarten, sit back in his child-sized recliner, throw his hands behind his head, and say, "Ah! It doesn't get better than this." Some time later, he would be ready to get up and go play or talk.

Early in his development, you will notice that the Introverted child is very content to play alone. He may go through a brief stage during which he quietly talks to himself about what he is doing, but soon that voice is internalized, and you will notice his quietness.

New people, situations, or events are not welcomed by the Introverted child. He greets them with caution and usually experiences them as an intrusion into his personal space. While on vacation in Hawaii with his family, a young Introvert was in tears on the third night at the thought of having to eat out again. "Why can't we eat at home (the hotel) tonight?" he'd cry. Frequently changing experiences can often distress an Introvert. An Introverted child may even perceive an Extraverted parent as an intrusion, especially if that parent doesn't understand the Introvert's need for quiet time alone.

He needs to observe before participating. An Extraverted parent may be disturbed by the Introverted child's tendency to wait for others to initiate activities, but this is perfectly normal. All too often, this hesitancy to join an activity is seen as a lack of enthusiasm. But if you observe the Introverted child carefully as he participates, you will see that, even though he is not enthusiastic at the beginning, his enthusiasm builds as he experiences the event. By the time the event is over, his enjoyment for it has emerged, and he may not want the activity to stop.

You need to remember that an Introverted child likes to observe things before he has to try them. For example, if he has to give an oral report in school, it is helpful if he doesn't have to go first; this gives him time to see what some of the other students are doing and allows him to better understand what he needs to do.

He is often seen as a shy child. The behaviors of the Introverted child can often be interpreted as shyness. This is not the case. Both Extraverted and Introverted children can be shy. A good way to test whether what you see in a child is introversion or shyness is to notice how he talks. Once a shy, Extraverted child is comfortable with you, he will talk a mile a minute, with very few pauses. In fact, as you listen you may wonder how or when he takes a breath. The Introverted child, whether he is shy or not, will usually speak with a number of pauses, almost as if he is waiting for his brain and his mouth to get back in sync with each other. Shyness in the Extraverted child can be very frustrating, for Extraverts want to be with other people and interact with them. But if an Extravert is shy, he battles within himself; usually the shyness wins out, and the Extravert withdraws in frustration. The Introverted child who is also shy will tend to withdraw from all interaction with other people. He may depend on one parent for all interactive issues, while avoiding any additional interaction, even with other family members. You won't see this in the Introvert who is not shy; he will interact easily with a select group of friends and family.

He doesn't need external affirmation as often or in the same ways that an Extraverted child does. External affirmations are not that important to the Introverted child. He tends to get his affirmation from within himself. For example, he may clean the kitchen while you're out and act like he hopes you don't even notice. When you thank him, he enjoys your appreciation as long as you don't overdo it. A simple thank-you is sufficient. His satisfaction comes from his awareness that he did something special. He only needs you to notice, but please don't make a big deal out of it. That's what the Extraverted child needs.

He doesn't have a great need for conversation. Long and/or deep conversations with an Introverted child will be sporadic. They will occur when the Introverted child has a need for them to occur. It's next to impossible for a parent to initiate these types of conversations with an Introverted child on a regular basis. It's best to be ready for them to happen at any time, and when they do, to treasure them. You can facilitate these conversations happening more often if you will allow the Introverted child to control the pace of the conversation. A parent's developing good listening skills will help the Introverted child feel more comfortable sharing with the parent more frequently over time.

When an Introvert looks like an Extravert and vice versa

Sometimes the Introverted child will look like an Extravert in that he talks a lot. Sometimes the Introvert will do this because he is nervous, but this usually takes place only around his closest couple of friends. You can't make the determination about Introversion/Extraversion by looking at the child's interaction with family or with a few select friends. You can't really see the difference there. You need to look at how he talks within a larger context—people outside the family or the circle of his two or three close friends. The Introvert numbers only a few people as "real friends," preferring to refer to the others as "friends, but. . . ."

In the same way, sometimes an Extraverted child will look like an Introvert, but this usually happens when he is totally worn out by all his activities. Illness or exhaustion can certainly take its toll on an Extravert. A normally talkative, active child can become quiet and inactive if he is not feeling well. After the prescribed treatment or rest, the child will return to his extraverted self.

Understanding Your Child Better

Photocopy these lists, using one set for each child. Put an *x* by the trait that is seen more often in each child:

THE EXTRAVERTED CHILD WILL MORE OFTEN	THE INTROVERTED CHILD WILL MORE OFTEN
○ relate primarily to an external world	○ relate primarily to an internal world
○ be comfortable with new places, people, and events/activities	○ want to understand or know people, places, and events/activities before experiencing them
○ talk while learning—he or she will talk a lot	○ think through things silently before talking
○ not be comfortable with solitude	○ need solitude/down-time regularly

○ need friends to play with   ○ be content to play alone

○ thrive on external validation   ○ not depend on external validation

○ be easily distracted   ○ be good at concentration

○ find silence frustrating   ○ find silence comfortable

As you consider each of your children, list their names below and then write after each name either the letter *E* or the letter *I* to indicate whether you think that child is an Extravert or an Introvert.

Talk with your spouse and your child's grandparents to see if you all agree or to help determine the dominant preference of a child who seems to exhibit traits of both preferences.

CHILD'S NAME   PREFERENCE

_____   _____

_____   _____

_____   _____

_____   _____

_____   _____

_____   _____

THE SENSING CHILD

This child gathers information about life through her five senses.

She prefers the concrete rather than the abstract. Like Sensing adults, a Sensing child likes concrete things that can be seen, heard, smelled, tasted, or touched. This type of child lives in the present and likes real things—real stories about real people. As a result, she likes things to be specific and precise. If you are giving a Sensing child directions, she wants them to be clear and concrete. For example, the direction "Clean your room" is very concrete, but not very specific. The Sensing child will tend to work at cleaning her room at a steady pace until she finishes the task. If cleaning the room involves throwing things away, the Sensing child quickly makes a decision and out it goes.

Her thinking tends to be linear; she is good at following specific, sequential steps. When the Sensing child is in the preschool stage, you will notice that she plays with a specific toy the way it was designed to be played with, rather than turning it to other "creative" uses. As this child enters elementary school, she likes to follow step-by-step instructions. As she works on a homework problem that is difficult, she will go back through the steps again to review, making certain she understands. She tends to comprehend the completed project—the general picture—by starting with the specifics. If the assignment hasn't been spelled out in detail, she will need help conceptualizing the finished product in a way that will help her know where to begin. When faced with a similar problem in the future, she will tend to use the tried-and-true methods of problem solving that worked before. "If it worked before, it should work again" is the Sensing child's motto.

She is good at grasping and memorizing facts. The Sensing child's attention to detail makes memorizing facts easy for her. She not only likes memorizing facts, she maintains a good, long-term memory of what she has memorized. She likes tests that are based on facts and that can be learned by rote. Open-ended questions are meaningless to her.

▶▶ **An iNtuitive mother had previously taught the English literature class her eleventh-grade Sensing daughter was now taking. Her daughter brought home a practice test. As the mother looked over her daughter's work, she saw that question 14 had been skipped. The mother realized that this question was one she had written when she taught the course. She asked her daughter why she had skipped the question, and the daughter answered, "It's a stupid question." It was to the Sensing child, for it was an open-ended question that asked "How else could the story have ended?" To the Sensing child, a story ends the way it ends—that's all there is to it.**

As a child develops her Sensing preferences, each time something is experienced she is gathering data. Gradually, a memory chain is established so that eventually something is mastered. For example, the Sensing child will go over and over multiplication tables until a memory chain is established. Over time, the child is able to internalize the multiplication tables and quickly access any data that is needed without taking too much thought on the subject. The abstract ideas about multiplication are confusing to the Sensing child, and trying to get her to understand the abstract doesn't help her learn.

A Sensing child reads everything in a story. She tends to begin on page 1 and continue until she finishes the book. She likes short adventure stories, biographies, and books of data like the *Guinness Book of World Records*. She also likes to read the directions. If a teacher's directions aren't clear or a step has been left out, it is the Sensing child who will interrupt and ask specific questions to help the teacher fill in what was left out in the assignment. A Sensing child also likes to focus on specific skills. It's not enough to tell a young Sensing son who is helping his father around the house to "just put that switch plate back on." The Sensing child wants his father to tell him step-by-step *how* to put the switch plate back on the wall.

THE INTUITIVE CHILD

This child uses his five senses but will draw conclusions from data he receives through his sixth sense—his intuition.

He is comfortable with the abstract. Many times an iNtuitive child is not even aware of using his five senses to gather information. He seems to think that he "just knows." He will also tend to focus on the future, talking more about what we "might" do next weekend than about what we are doing right now.

Giving an iNtuitive child directions may not be enough. The response to "clean your room" may only last a few moments. The iNtuitive child begins to clean up his room, but one of the items he picks up to put away sparks his imagination. Toys that have been strewn across his desk suddenly captivate his attention, and play interrupts the cleaning of the room. An hour later only three things have been picked up, for he's been distracted by the fourth thing he started to put away. The iNtuitive child seldom throws anything away, for who knows what use it might have in the future. What the iNtuitive child often needs is very short directions, such as "Put your books on this shelf, and put this toy in this box" or for the parent to stay and supervise the project.

He is bored by linear thinking. As a preschooler, the iNtuitive child may ignore the obvious ways to play with toys but will play with them in ways the toy maker never even imagined. Or something that isn't even a toy becomes a favorite thing to play with. A funny-shaped branch suddenly becomes an airplane, or a blanket stretched across a couple of chairs becomes a tent on the prairie in the Wild West.

▶▶ **A two-and-a-half-year-old iNtuitive child was fascinated with the vacuum cleaner. He liked the noise it made. When told he couldn't plug the sweeper into the electrical outlet, he proceeded to "plug it in" between the cushions on the couch and then pushed it, making his own vacuum-cleaner noise. His fascination with the sweeper lasted for several months, and he left most of his toys alone during that time.**

Factual tests need to be taken quickly by the iNtuitive child, partly because if he labors over a question too long, he will see too many possible answers and probably get it wrong. He much prefers open-ended questions such as "How else could the story have ended?" He can write pages about "what might have been." Memorization of facts is difficult for him to stick with. When he is working on memorizing the multiplication tables, he will continually sidetrack himself by looking for patterns. He may learn the nines by noticing that the sum always adds up to nine, and that each time the second number decreases by one, the first number increases by one.

In school, the iNtuitive child will often stop listening to directions before they are completed. He often believes that he knows what the teacher is going to say, so why keep listening? If the iNtuitive child has grasped the bigger picture of the assignment, he will be able to do it without all the specific directions. But he may take off on the project, jumping ahead of the teacher, and find out later he was not going where the teacher was going.

Imagination is a key word for the iNtuitive child. He loves the world of ideas. Facts are boring. Sometimes he plays with an idea so much that he never gets around to actually doing anything with it. A school project may trigger a number of ideas, and most of the time allowed for the project is spent thinking through each of those ideas. As a result, by the time the iNtuitive child gets around to doing the project, time has almost run out, and he has to downsize his earlier idea.

He starts with the big picture, then moves to specifics. When solving problems, the iNtuitive child will usually begin with the bigger picture and then fill in some of the specifics. Too many specifics can be boring, and too much routine must be avoided. If the iNtuitive child has solved a problem one way, why do it the same way next time? "Let's see if there's another way to solve this" might be his attitude. This is true for school projects or even which route he takes home from school. If something triggers his imagination, he might be inspired to try another way home, even if it's longer.

The iNtuitive child loves to read but often skims over what has been "assigned" to be read. He will especially skim over parts that are too detailed. He loves to read novels and especially science fiction. His imagination is so engaged that stories about exotic places or times can transport him thousands of miles away and hundreds of years into the past or the future. Playing Let's Pretend as a young child will keep his attention for long periods of time. Daydreaming of some magical kingdom can be a favorite pastime.

Understanding Your Child Better

Photocopy these lists, using one set for each child. Put an *x* by the trait that is seen more often in each child:

THE SENSING CHILD WILL MORE OFTEN	THE INTUITIVE CHILD WILL MORE OFTEN
○ be very concrete and specific	○ be more abstract, live in a world of ideas
○ play with toys as designed	○ play imaginatively with toys
○ love facts	○ love to daydream (facts are boring)
○ memorize easily	○ find it hard to focus on specifics
○ read slower but grasp details	○ read quickly and skim material
○ want step-by-step instructions	○ be impatient with instructions
○ start with specifics and move to the big picture	○ start with the big picture and move to specifics

As you consider each of your children, list their names below and then write after each name either the letter S or the letter N to indicate whether you think that child is Sensing or iNtuitive.

Talk with your spouse and your child's grandparents to see if you all agree or to help determine the dominant preference of a child who seems to exhibit traits of both preferences.

CHILD'S NAME   PREFERENCE

_____   _____

_____   _____

_____   _____

_____   _____

_____   _____

_____   _____

THE THINKING CHILD

This child makes decisions mainly through her intellect.

She makes detached, logical, and objective decisions. If your child prefers the Thinking function, she will want to analyze the information she has gathered and then decide— rationally—what to do. A favorite question of the Thinking child is "Why?" She asks this question because she needs to understand. If a parent tries to short-circuit the *why* with a "because I'm the parent and I said so," the Thinking child will simply stop asking why out loud. But she will still need to understand why.

She is analytical and good at understanding ideas. Thinking children have an affinity for classes such as science and math, where their analytical skills are put to effective use. They love to debate and will take up the challenge on either side if given the opportunity. For the Thinking child, intellectual competition is the stuff life is made of. She works very hard at being correct, and she needs for her effort to be respected by both parents and the teacher.

Sometimes this need to be right can get her into trouble, because she will appear to sacrifice a relationship for the sake of rightness. It's important to note the word *appear.* Her expertise at understanding ideas is almost nonexistent when it comes to understanding relationships. She simply

53

cannot understand how her "true" statement could cause hard feelings in a relationship.

▶▶ **A Thinking child was accompanying his Feeling friend, Bill, on an outing to Disneyland. In the car on the way there, the Feeling child was so excited he could hardly contain himself. He was jumping around in his seat and asking all kinds of questions about the day. The Thinking child sat quietly all the way there. His parents asked if he was excited about the day at Disneyland and he said, "I sure am. I'm just as excited as Bill."**

The emotional side of the Thinking child certainly exists, even though she does not say much about those feelings. You will probably see some emotion, though, whenever she fails at a task. Failure at anything, especially when seen by the larger group of peers, can be devastating. On the other side, the way a Thinking child may show emotions, such as love, is to do a good job. The A's on the report card are a sign of her caring for her parents and the rest of the family.

She prefers to work on individual projects as opposed to group projects. Working individually gives her the ability to evaluate her own performance, which she does quite accurately. When a parent offers praise to a Thinking child, it needs to be very specific. To say to a Thinking child that something she did "was great!" is meaningless. She wants to know what it was about what she did that was so great. When the Thinking child asks the parent, "Why did you think that was so great?" the parent needs to list the specifics. To simply repeat the generalized statement negates the compliment the parent is trying to give to the Thinking child.

A word of caution about bringing up a Thinking daughter
Because only one-third of girls are Thinkers, some parents
become concerned when their daughters show an interest
in technical classes. This interest is merely an indication
that she is a Thinker.

If the Thinking girl is going to continue her academic
success after she discovers boys, she will need a lot of
affirmation in earlier grades from both parents for her
so-called masculine classroom interests such as science.
In fact, the Thinking daughter will need extra affirmation
during the elementary grades simply because her interests
may be so different from her Feeling mom or from the
majority of other girls. A parent's understanding of this
preference in the Thinking daughter will go a long way in
preserving her confident sense of self, especially as she
enters puberty.

Games give a great deal of insight into whether a child
is Thinking or Feeling. For the Thinking child, rules are
extremely important. Even before a child is old enough to
really understand the rules of a game, the emerging Thinking child will be talking about the "rules." At an early age,
the rules may change often, but the rules are important.
For the Feeling child, rules are secondary to relationships.
If a rule is going to eliminate someone from the game, the
Feeling child may suggest that an exception to the rule be
made. She doesn't want her friend to not be able to play.

THE FEELING CHILD
This child makes decisions through subjective personal
values and by how the decision will affect relationships.

**He makes subjective decisions that take into account
the feelings of others.** If your child prefers the Feeling
function, he will base decisions on his personal values and

on the impact any decision will have on friends and family members. Rather than worry about the *whys* of a situation, the Feeling child will be concerned about the other people in that situation. His question will be something like "Will this upset anyone?"

If a Feeling child knows that his parents are likely to answer "just because I said so," the fact that the mere question could upset them causes the child to refrain from even asking why. Or if he does ask why and receives "just because" as an answer, he won't question further. More important than learning the *why* is pleasing the other person.

Thus, a Feeling child's concern about the feelings of others means that he will often find it difficult to say what he means. He evaluates his thoughts and opinions and softens them as he speaks.

The Feeling child usually cannot give reasons for his decisions or opinions. Sometimes it helps to teach him how to use objective skills, such as making a pro-and-con list or talking to a very logical friend who can raise objective issues, when he makes decisions. But the final act of making a decision must never be made at the expense of what his subjective experience is telling him.

▶▶ **A sixteen-year-old Feeling daughter was given the task of buying a car. Both her parents were Thinking types. When the Feeling daughter told them she had found a blue VW Rabbit, they started listing the things she needed to do before she bought the car, such as comparative shopping, having two or three other cars to inspect, etc. Finally, in tears, the Feeling daughter said, "But I want the blue one with the white rabbit painted on the side."**

Praise is important to him. He is more dependent upon external affirmations than is a Thinking child. If the teacher doesn't praise the good work the Feeling child has done, that child may think the teacher doesn't like him anymore. Oversights are taken personally by the Feeling child, and he has a difficult time trying to be objective about those types of things. Ten positive compliments about an action done by a Feeling child will be completely negated by one negative criticism. Criticism can be devastating to a Feeling child. When disciplining the Feeling child, a harsh look from the parent may be all that is needed for the child to feel more than adequately punished. If criticism becomes ridicule on the playground, the Feeling child may find it impossible to recover and may withdraw into a protective shell of isolation.

He is good at understanding people. From an early age, the Feeling child is gifted in his ability to understand other people. He can feel the discomfort of the new kid in the classroom, and during recess he may make the effort to help that child assimilate into his group of friends. In the same way, the Feeling child can quickly sense the emotional atmosphere in the home, sometimes even becoming physically ill because of the tension the parents are experiencing. As a result, this child will work very hard in social situations to keep things harmonious.

He is easier to "read" than a Thinking child. His emotional responses are usually written all over his face. He may try to hide his feelings but finds it difficult to do so. He tends to cry more easily than the Thinking child, who may sometimes will himself *not* to show any emotional reactions when corrected by a parent or a teacher.

Competition is not that important to him. Feeling children are usually not very competitive. They understand that for them to win, someone else has to lose. Their winning at something can be spoiled by the realization that someone else lost. They may even apologize for winning, which is totally absurd to the Thinking child.

The Feeling child will enjoy working on group projects in school. Success will be based not only on the grade received but also on how well the small group enjoyed working together. In fact, the Feeling child may feel particularly good about the fact that everyone in the group got the same grade and that they were able to help some of the lower-achieving members of the group get a better grade than they would have achieved on their own.

A word of caution about bringing up a Feeling son

When boys prefer the Feeling function, it can be especially hard on them because of their sensitivity. Unless the father, who may be a Thinking person, can affirm his son's preference for Feeling, the young boy may grow up trying to hide his sensitive side and experience all kinds of internal conflicts.

The Feeling son's interest in art or music or even literature needs to be affirmed by both parents, but especially by the father. If the father is afraid that the son will have too difficult a time growing up so sensitive, he needs to understand that the best thing he can do for this son is to affirm his natural bent. When a father can do this, the son usually does exceptionally well as an adult, for success in using the Feeling function is built on self-confidence, not on being "tough."

It is important to remember that both the Thinking child and the Feeling child have equal amounts of feelings or emotions. But the Feeling child is more comfortable talking about or showing his emotions than the Thinking child is. Family trauma will affect both types of children. But because the Thinking child does not show his feelings, parents may believe that the child is coping quite well with what is going on. The highly emotional responses of the Feeling child may cause parents to believe that it is the Feeling child that needs help coping. The truth will be somewhere in between—both will need help coping, and the Thinking child may need more help in learning how to express what he is feeling on the inside.

Understanding Your Child Better

Photocopy these lists, using one set for each child. Put an *x* by the trait that is seen more often in each child:

THE THINKING CHILD WILL MORE OFTEN	THE FEELING CHILD WILL MORE OFTEN
○ love the why questions	○ be more concerned with others' feelings
○ be very objective	○ be very subjective
○ love to debate with you	○ not want to hurt you, so won't debate
○ love competition	○ treat competition as secondary to relationships
○ fight to be right	○ be good at understanding people and negotiating
○ like individual projects	○ like group projects
○ enjoy analyzing things	○ show feelings on own face
○ treat rules as primary in games	○ treat people's feelings as primary in games

As you consider each of your children, list their names below and then write after each name either the letter *T* or the letter *F* to indicate whether you think that child is a Thinker or a Feeler.

Talk with your spouse and your child's grandparents to see if you all agree or to help determine the dominant preference of a child who seems to exhibit traits of both preferences.

CHILD'S NAME   PREFERENCE

_____   _____

_____   _____

_____   _____

_____   _____

_____   _____

_____   _____

THE JUDGING CHILD

This child is an organizer of her world.

She will learn early to prepare for tasks. She's a good budgeter of time so that she can finish early and avoid the pressure of coming up against a deadline. She will also take great pride in the finished product. Parents who are open-ended or who constantly change their plans can frustrate the Judging child by their lack of decisiveness. The Judging child likes things settled in advance so that she can anticipate what is going to happen.

Too many tasks given at about the same time can also frustrate the Judging child, for she likes to have closure on everything that has been assigned. If she can't get everything finished, she will be easily discouraged and stressed. Giving the Judging child one task at a time helps her enjoy her ability to finish things.

Her gift of organization can also lead the Judging child to think it is her job to get everyone else in the household similarly organized.

▶▶ **A Perceiving parent was describing her eleven-year-old Judging daughter with great pride. The parent told about how organized her daughter was and how helpful she was around the house. "In fact," the mother said, "my daughter is so organized that by the time I leave my bedroom in the morning, she already has a list posted on my bedroom door of what *I* need to do that day."**

She works best where rules are clear and predictable. The Judging child works best in a home or classroom where the rules are clear and predictable, where schedules and routines are clearly defined, and where changes in any of these areas are minimal or nonexistent. From an early age, Judging children tend to be neat and orderly. They like their stuffed animals lined up a certain way, their socks arranged in the right drawer, and their clothes on hangers. When they start school, their notebooks will be neat and orderly, with all extraneous papers tucked neatly into a pocket inside the cover.

Rules are very important to the Judging child. She wants to know what the rules are so she can follow them. If another child breaks a rule, the Judging child will often tell the teacher. She may be seen as a tattletale, but what the Judging child is doing by telling the teacher is checking to see if the rule is still in force. If the other child can break the rule without a consequence, then maybe the rule doesn't exist anymore, and the Judging child can also break it.

Like the Judging adult, she has a work ethic about life. The task must be done before she can play. So chores are done either on time or early, and homework is done first. Tasks that are assigned by a parent to a Judging child are done promptly, to the parent's delight, regardless of the child's own preferences. On the other hand, being told to "get to bed" before she has finished what she is doing will create tension within the Judging child that will make sleep very slow in coming. The unfinished task will keep her awake with worry.

A Judging child is very time conscious. If one of the parents is late picking up the car pool, the Judging child will become very uncomfortable on the days when that parent drives. If the child is also a Thinking child, she may say to the driver, "I like to be early for school so I can get ready for my first class. Would you please see that you are on time the next time you drive?" This type of child likes to be early to things and respects adults who have the same preference. It is very difficult for her to feel that an adult who is always late has any respect for her.

THE PERCEIVING CHILD

This child organizes his world in creative ways.

He usually finds too many rules to be restrictive. The close proximity of a deadline for a school assignment creates the energy for him to tackle the task, even though internally he may have been thinking about what he needed to do all along. Changes in schedule are welcomed by the Perceiving child, since it gives him a sense of having some options. Options are very important to the Perceiving child, so much so that too many rules may even cause him to break the rules. Sometimes he breaks a rule simply because his spontaneity overrides his ability to think about what he is doing. Other times, he breaks a rule simply because he is indifferent to it or feels that it applies to other children but not to him. Or he may believe that a rule is no longer in force, because yesterday a Judging child observed a teacher failing to enforce that particular rule!

He gives little appearance of being organized. When looking at the room of the Perceiving child, one wonders how he finds anything. But unless Mother has just cleaned the room, the Perceiving child can quickly find whatever he needs in the midst of obvious chaos. His school notebook will be filled with papers that appear to have no order to them. There are loose pages tucked in everywhere. But ask the Perceiving child for a particular sheet, and he knows right where it is.

Rather than having the external world organized as the Judging child does, the Perceiving child has what appears to be an internal sense of order that has no apparent rhyme or reason to others.

He likes life to be open-ended. His love of the spontaneous can often frustrate a parent, regardless of whether the parent's preference is Judging or Perceiving. At bedtime the Perceiving child suddenly remembers that tomorrow he is supposed to bring the cupcakes for a class party. Or at the dinner table, the seventeen-year-old Perceiving adolescent tells Dad that he needs the car tonight for a date.

The reason even the Perceiving parent can be frustrated by these kinds of requests is that parenting is often geared to training a child in the skills of a Judging person. So the parent who has ten unfinished needlepoints in her closet will insist that the Perceiving child finish something and clean up the mess before starting something else. Or the parent whose bedroom closet is in a constant state of disorder feels that, as a good parent, she must get her Perceiving child to straighten out the mess in *his* closet. These inconsistencies are usually not noticed by the parent until the child points them out, and then they are overlooked because neatness and order are what any parent is supposed to teach a child. There is truth to this, but the Perceiving child needs to be encouraged to develop his own sense of order.

▶▶ **One of our sons is a Judging type, and his older brother by one year is a Perceiving type. All through elementary school they shared a room. At first, the way the Judging son coped with his Perceiving brother's messiness was to draw a line between their beds and make sure the mess never crossed the line. Later on, the Perceiving son paid his Judging brother to clean up his side of the room once a week.**

He's a charmer. The Perceiving child is very winsome and can be quite entertaining in a family. His love of spontaneous play can be infectious. He is able to enter completely into what is happening now and have fun. Part of the reason he enjoys life so much is that he is much more oriented to the process of doing something than he is to the finished product. The fun is in the doing—in the process.

Time is relative to the Perceiving child. A Perceiving child seems to have a knack for being where he is supposed to be at the right time, but watching him can give the other person ulcers. He has a very relaxed approach to time, which even shows itself when you ask him, "What time is it?" "Almost noon" might be his answer, even though he looks at his watch and sees that it is 11:50. In contrast, when you ask a Judging child what time it is, he will usually tell you, and want you to tell him if he asks, the precise time.

You can never give a Perceiving child too many tasks. He can let his assigned chores pile up, and it doesn't bother him at all. He may work on them a little at a time, moving between one task and another. The job of washing the dishes after dinner can turn into a half hour of soapsuds sculpturing. And while he is doing the dishes, he may stop and watch a TV program, start something else, and then just before Mom gets really upset, finish the dishes.

He is working even when he appears not to be. This is why, when a deadline looms close, he is able to do a lot in a short period of time. This can make the Judging parent wonder what the Perceiving child might accomplish if he would ever get organized. But his personal sense of order is what allows him to get things done quickly.

What others often fail to see is that, internally, the Perceiving child may be working on a project while he is playing. For example, if he has to give an oral presentation in class tomorrow, he has been thinking about it off and on since the assignment was given. He may not even know for sure what he's going to talk about until a few minutes before the teacher calls on him. But when he gives the oral presentation, he gets an A. If we only look at the externals, we may think that he hasn't prepared and that his A is somehow a fluke. We haven't been able to observe the internal preparation that has been going on at various times while he was doing something else.

Understanding Your Child Better

Photocopy these lists, using one set for each child. Put an *x* by the trait that is seen more often in each child:

THE JUDGING CHILD WILL MORE OFTEN	THE PERCEIVING CHILD WILL MORE OFTEN
○ prepare for tasks	○ give little outward appearance of organization
○ work best with clear, predictable rules	○ find too many rules to be restrictive
○ have a good work ethic	○ play at any time and anywhere
○ be very time conscious	○ find time to be relative, not specific
○ have a sense of order in own room	○ have no outward sense of order regarding room
○ be uncomfortable with change	○ be able to handle change well
○ take pride in the finished product	○ be very charming with other people
○ work methodically	○ work quickly in spurts

As you consider each of your children, list their names below and then write after each name either the letter *J* or the letter *P* to indicate whether you think that child is a Judger or a Perceiver.

Talk with your spouse and your child's grandparents to see if you all agree or to help determine the dominant preference of a child who seems to exhibit traits of both preferences.

CHILD'S NAME   PREFERENCE

_____   _____

_____   _____

_____   _____

_____   _____

_____   _____

Now that you have looked at each of the pairs of traits and have decided which set of four traits each of your children prefers, write their names and the letters for each of the four preferences you feel represents their personalities. Because we will look at how these preferences interact with each other in the following chapters, it is important that you identify as best you can the preferences of your children. If you're not certain about a specific preference, read on, and maybe the next chapters will help to clear up your choices.

Your child's name   E or I   S or N   T or F   J or P
(For example: Jan   E N F P)

CHILD'S NAME   PREFERENCES

_____   _____

_____   _____

_____   _____

_____   _____

_____   _____

_____   _____

CHAPTER FOUR

From Personality Preferences to Basic Temperaments

We've looked at the individual preferences in our own personalities as well as those in the personalities of our children. At the end of the last chapter, you were able to identify the four preferences of each of your children. Each letter combination of the four preferences works out to one of the sixteen different possible personality styles.

LEARNING TO WATCH AND LISTEN FOR PERSONALITY CLUES

As we've described each of the four pairs of preferences, we hope we have helped you become better people watchers or, more accurately, better "personality listeners." You are now able to listen to people talk and tell whether they are Introverts or Extraverts. You know that Introverts often pause as they talk. Some say they do this so that their brain and their mouth can get back into sync with each other. And you know that Extraverts talk; words just seem to tumble out. Sometimes you wonder if they ever take a breath.

You can also listen for the differences between Sensing people and iNtuitive people. Sensing people tend to speak in complete thoughts, finishing sentences, whereas iNtuitive people seldom finish a thought without introducing another thought. Often, the iNtuitive person will suddenly shift ideas in the middle of a sentence, skipping quickly to another thought.

Thinking people often use "thinking"-type words that describe a rational process, whereas Feeling people often use "feeling"-type words that describe an emotional reaction. For example, if you ask a Feeling person, "What do you *think* about . . . ?" that person will almost always answer, "Well, I *feel* that. . . ." In the same way, if you ask a Thinking person, "What do you *feel* about . . . ?" that person will almost always answer, "Well, I *think* that. . . ." Paying attention to a person's choice of words can help us understand whether that person is a Thinking person or a Feeling person.

When it comes to the Judging or Perceiving preference, we become "people watchers." We can notice that a Perceiving person feels boxed in by having her day planned too tightly in advance. In her spontaneity, she is not bothered too much by many things happening around her; she can be flexible with it. The Judging person often feels at loose ends because he has a block of time that isn't planned out in advance. He needs closure on one thing before starting another.

FROM SIXTEEN COMBINATIONS TO FOUR TEMPERAMENTS

What is interesting about these sixteen possible personalities is that if we consider how these preferences interact with each other, we can group the sixteen combinations of preferences into four temperaments.

These four temperaments were first identified by David Keirsey and Marilyn Bates. In their research, they observed that those with the Sensing preference showed marked differences in their personalities based on whether they had chosen the Judging preference or the Perceiving preference. This led the researchers to identify two temperaments as being the SP temperament and the SJ temperament.

What made a difference in those who preferred the iNtuitive trait was whether they preferred the Thinking function or the Feeling function. Keirsey and Bates identified these other two temperaments as the NF temperament and the NT temperament.

Based on these differences, the researchers were able to define and describe four basic temperaments.[2] They called them temperaments to distinguish them from personality.

The preference for Introversion and Extraversion did not affect any of these choices, except in how well we can observe the particular temperament in each child. The Introverted SP child will be very much like the Extraverted SP child, except that the Introvert, being focused primarily on the internal world, will not show the SP characteristics as quickly as the Extravert will. We need to be observers, and we need time to see them. As we look through each of these four temperaments, we will see how the Introversion/Extraversion preference might affect each particular temperament.

Understanding Your Child Better

To see which temperament you, your spouse, and each of your children represent, first find the column in the chart

[2] For more information on how these temperaments were developed, see *Please Understand Me* by David Keirsey and Marilyn Bates (Prometheus Nemesis, 1978).

below that contains the four letters that represent your four
preferences. Then write down your first name under the
column below your four-letter combination. Do the same
with your spouse, writing down his or her name below the
column containing his or her four letters. Then do the same
with the names of each of your children.

Above each column of four-letter combinations is a two-
letter combination. These are the letters designating the
temperament defined by each four-letter combination.
For example, if one of your children is an ESFP, you would
write her name under the column that is headed by SP.
Or if one of your children is an INTJ, you would write his
name under the NT column.

SP	SJ	NT	NF
ESFP	ESFJ	ENTJ	ENFJ
ESTP	ESTJ	ENTP	ENFP
ISFP	ISFJ	INTJ	INFJ
ISTP	ISTJ	INTP	INFP
___	___	___	___
___	___	___	___
___	___	___	___
___	___	___	___
___	___	___	___
___	___	___	___

In our earlier discussion, we noted that we have all eight traits within us to some degree. No one has completely and exclusively one trait as opposed to its polar opposite. That's why we call them "preferences." Therefore, it also stands to reason that no one will be totally and exclusively one temperament. Since we have some of all the traits within us, we may also sometimes exhibit (as will our children) behaviors that represent some of the other temperaments.

But we will begin to better understand these temperaments if we see that one of them is going to be our "home"; it is the place where we spend most of our time. These letters are not labels. They simply identify what we are *most* of the time. One of them will describe most of what we do and who we are. And it is this temperament that we will "assign" to ourselves or to each of our children as the "basic" temperament. Keep this in mind as you look at yourself and at each of your children.

We become more adept at understanding our child's personality if we first understand our own personality and that of our spouse. To get started, let's look at each of these temperaments in terms of us as adults. Then in the chapters that follow we will look at how they play out in our children.

THE SENSING/PERCEIVING (SP) TEMPERAMENT
THE INDIVIDUALISTS AND THE PLAYERS

If you are an SP, you make up about 37 percent of the population in our country. You are an Individualist if you are an Introvert and a Player if you are an Extravert. You are the prototypical "today" person. Today must be enjoyed! Duty, power, and growth are all secondary issues. *Action* is the key to a life well lived. Action is an end in itself to the SP, seldom a means to another end, unless that also involves some kind of action. The SP can be impatient and hates to wait.

The SP's desire for action is seen in his reaction to an activity called "practice." SPs never practice, for that is simply preparation for something happening in the future. They simply *do*. Another way of saying it is that their practice *is* the performance, and they perform very well.

We had a friend who was a major league baseball player—a pitcher. His son was also very good at baseball and was pitching for his high school team. The son was an SP who practiced when the team did, but that was the only time he practiced. It was only when his father understood the SP's attitude toward practice that he allowed his son to be himself. Prior to that, he was always on his son's back, urging him to practice more, and his son was always finding excuses to not practice his pitching. To the son, practice took place the day he was supposed to perform, during the game when he was pitching. And he, like other SPs, usually did it very well.

The SP's love for action is closely linked to the need to be free to act. "Don't take away my options," he will say strongly. Or "Don't fence me in!" As a result, he is often seen as free spirited and independent. SPs are often misunderstood, especially SPs who are introverted. They have the same craving for action the extravert has, but others don't often see it. Instead, the introverted SP is seen as restless, easily bored, and, of course, not very disciplined.

A job that requires an SP to sit at a desk in an office for eight hours a day can be like a slow death to him. So SP men are drawn to jobs that are outdoors, such as construction or trucking. Tools and heavy equipment are fascinating to the SP. SP women are often drawn to sales or interior design professions. When we presented our seminar to a large group of Air Force personnel, we found that the only SPs in the audience were fighter pilots. They loved living on the edge and taking calculated risks. If an SP is in the medical profession, surgery, or the emergency room with their constant challenges, will keep him interested. Working as a firefighter or a paramedic provides the same variety of activities and action for the SP. He also has an affinity for the crisis and is well equipped to respond quickly and effectively to emergencies.

Some SPs are drawn to the arts as performers, artists, or interior designers. If they are drawn to nursing, the emergency room will keep them from being bored. Sometimes they get into teaching and almost always end up teaching kindergarten, the arts, or physical education. Or they get into a small business such as a beauty salon, pizza shop, or real-estate office, seeking the independence of working for themselves.

One thing SPs will not spend much, if any, time with is the *Standard Operating Procedures* manual. They work best by ignoring the procedures and solving the problem. "Just tell me what to do—don't tell me how to do it" is their motto. Both men and women will be frustrated by the corporation and its limitations on personal freedom to act as well as its emphasis on procedures. They may serve in a corporate position for several years and then end up working as a consultant. Their love for troubleshooting makes them excellent consultants.

I remember meeting an SP who was an engineer. As I expressed my amazement that he was in that field of work, he quickly pointed out that his job was to try and break what the other engineers were producing. He was fortunate in that his company found an effective way to use his natural abilities as well as his training.

I was also curious as to how an SP engineer had made it through college, for SPs are not usually motivated by higher education. They would much rather just get out there and do what they want to do. When I asked this SP engineer about his college experience, he acknowledged the struggle he had had. He said that in his family there had been no choice about going to college, and when he was in college, there was little choice about what to major in. If you were a male, you studied engineering. "And," he added, "math was just naturally easy for me, so that helped."

SPs experience only temporary defeat. They survive setbacks with what seems to other types apparent ease. Their ability to do this is enhanced by their tendency to hold on to things loosely. If something is lost, they might say, "Oh well, something else will come along." In addition, hardship is seen as a challenge or an adventure. SPs are not working toward some goal in the far-off future; they are living a here-and-now adventure. Life is not seen as getting better when the problem is solved—nothing could be better than the problem-solving adventure of right now. Their sense of optimism will keep them focused on the adventure long after other types have given up and gone home.

THE SENSING/JUDGING (SJ) TEMPERAMENT
THE ORGANIZERS AND THE MONITORS

If you are an SJ, you make up about 39 percent of the population in our country. You are an Organizer if you are an Extravert and a Monitor if you are an Introvert. For you, *duty* is the word that best describes what makes you tick. You long to do your duty and be useful to society, your family, your church, your spouse, and especially to your children.

Closely paralleling this need to be useful is the need to belong. The SJ earns this sense of belonging through her desire to be a caretaker. Whereas the SP longs to be free to act, the SJ feels duty bound and obligated.

School, especially at elementary and secondary levels, is ideal for SJs. Most teachers in these grades are SJs, as are most administrators. They love to work on lesson plans. Teaching the same thing year after year is not a problem since they love to improve what they are already doing. School is one of the major institutions of our culture, so they are acting very responsibly if they are involved in some way within the school system.

This same sense of duty is seen in the adult in any organization, such as the women's church social or the men's breakfast, where SJs volunteer to help serve the food and then offer to stay afterward and help clean up. If they are involved in planning the event, they take care of all the details willingly and efficiently.

Our major league baseball friend is an SJ. Practice came naturally to him. He practiced with the team, and he dedicated time in his schedule to practice on his own. That was why it was so hard for him to understand his SP son. "One can never practice enough," he said to me, "especially if he wants to do well." After all, that's what he was supposed to do. And SJs always seem to know what they are supposed to do in any given situation.

SJs are always prepared. This sense of preparedness is what led some SJ men to create and organize the Boy Scouts. Their motto, "Be Prepared," is also every SJ's motto in life. Ask an SJ woman for something, and she probably has it in her purse. In Aesop's fable "The Ant and the Grasshopper," the hardworking ant was obviously an SJ. In the same way, the Proverb urging us all to "take a lesson from the ants" (Proverbs 6:6) is urging us to consider and incorporate the values of the SJ—the values of hard work and a strong sense of duty.

The famous Murphy of Murphy's Law was also an SJ.

He demonstrated the pessimistic streak SJs have—the pessimism that birthed Murphy's law: "Whatever can go wrong will go wrong." Whenever something does go wrong, SJs go instantly to the *Standard Operating Procedures* manual, which one of them probably wrote. The problem for SJs occurs when the procedures don't work. Then they are at a loss about what to do next. Instead of trying something new, they will usually just try over and over to get the procedure to work. Eventually they will call in the problem solver—the SP consultant—to fix what the procedures can't fix.

Jobs that require a lot of procedures are a pleasant challenge to most SJs. Therefore, they thrive in the corporate world as well as in the military. Administrators, secretaries, production and distribution people, bankers, or any other type of worker that is the cornerstone of our society or of an institution—all are havens for SJs.

Routines are welcomed by SJs. In fact, they like the predictability of knowing what to do next. They feel secure in jobs that require a high degree of repetition. Doing the same thing over and over again feels useful because it obviously works. What is very unsettling to SJs is unpredictability or having things change simply because someone wanted a change.

The SJs' need to take care of others often draws them to medical professions. Hospital staff, lab technicians, most nurses, and many doctors are SJs. Patient care is their primary concern, but following the right procedures runs a close second. The responsibility that goes with patient care is gladly accepted by SJs. In fact, they will often take on more responsibility than they can handle. And about the only way they can get out of a responsibility is to get ill.

But just being sick won't keep them home—that's too irresponsible. They have to be *very* sick.

Traditions are very important to SJs. Birthdays and holidays may be celebrated with a flourish, and traditions are carefully followed. The only change allowed is to expand on a tradition; seldom will SJs eliminate a tradition. Continuity with the past is extremely important to them. As a result, SJs are often seen as "pillars of society" (or of the church) or as "steady as a rock." SJs tend to always know how to do the right thing at the right time.

The Intuitive/Thinking (NT) Temperament
The Competitors and the Explorers

If you are an NT, you make up only 12 percent of the population in this country. You are a Competitor if you are an Extravert and an Explorer if you are an Introvert. In a large classroom of thirty-two children, only four would be NTs and only one would be an Introverted NT. If you are an NT, this may explain why you so often felt that you didn't fit in in a classroom where twenty-four kids were either SJs or SPs and the teacher and principal were most likely SJs as well.

If *action* is the word for the SP and *duty* is the word for the SJ, *competency* is the word for the NT. You won't see this immediately with the NT. What you will notice is that he is fascinated with power. But it is important to understand that he is fascinated with power not because he wants to be powerful but because power is a means to being more competent. More than anything else, the NT is driven by the need to be competent.

In order to be competent, one must always be improving. Therefore, everything NTs do, whether it is work or play, involves this drive to improve—to be even more competent. If you play tennis with an NT, be prepared for a tennis lesson. It's not that you play badly; it's just that the NT is giving himself a tennis lesson, and he wants to share the lesson with you. Play is never simply play. In fact, the NT often needs to schedule play just as he would schedule a business appointment. After all, one must play competently just as one must work and think competently.

Others are often put off by the intensity of NTs. They are very self-critical, but those around them will often feel this self-criticism as criticism of themselves. There is some truth to this, but in reality, NTs are simply concerned that others should at least try. They don't have to be competent as long as they try. A vague sense of failure, a strong drive toward perfectionism, and the feeling that one has never learned enough—all haunt the inner world of NTs.

When it comes to work, both male and female NTs are drawn toward jobs that have to do with the creation or application of scientific principles. The various fields of science, technology, research and development, architecture, and teaching in college or graduate school are all vocations that draw a high percentage of NTs. Philosophy and higher math are also attractive to NTs. In fact, most NTs are born philosophers. In a business, they lead with vision and are the ones who created the idea of "mission statements." After all, a mission statement defines a company's philosophy of doing business.

Redundancy is irritating to NTs. Therefore, they are often editing the *Standard Operating Procedures* manual—taking out all the redundant statements and policies. Words fascinate NTs. They love to play with words, creating verbal paradoxes, reading satire, and figuring out verbal puzzles.

The world of meaning for NTs lies in the future. But they also value the lessons of the past. A typical statement of an

NT would be "Fool me once, shame on you. Fool me twice, shame on me." Using the lessons of the past, NTs self-correct because they are unwilling to ever repeat an error. After all, that would be redundant.

Because they often struggle with showing affection and they don't like to waste words, an NT might say to a spouse, "I love you, and that stands until I revoke it." A couple in one of our seminars offered this illustration: The wife said, "I don't think my husband has said 'I love you' more than five times in our thirty-five-year marriage." Her NT husband spoke up. "I've said it six times, and I can tell you each time I said it and why I said it."

The NT's objectivity about life often gives those close to him the feeling that he is simply watching life rather than experiencing it. This is due also to the NT's struggle to read the emotional responses and needs of other people. NTs can be very sensitive and emotionally connected in a marriage, but usually that has grown slowly and steadily over the years. It doesn't come easily to them.

THE INTUITIVE/FEELING (NF) TEMPERAMENT
THE RELATORS AND THE DREAMERS

If you are an NF, you also make up only 12 percent of the population in our country. You are a Relator if you are an Extravert and a Dreamer if you are an Introvert. In a classroom of thirty-two children, like the NT, there would only be four NFs, and one of them would be an Introvert. And if the NT feels as if she doesn't fit in with the twenty-four SJs and SPs, the NF feels like a complete alien around the other types.

Whereas we could define the other three temperaments with a key word, the NF personality almost defies description. The quest of an NF has been described by Keirsey as "one becomes oneself if and only if one does not." (Only an NF can understand this statement.) We could say that the key word for NFs is *becoming*, but then we need to define how the NFs would say that. Usually the response to a goal of "becoming" is to ask, "Become what?" But for NFs, the "what" of the becoming is meaningless. NFs are in search of growth; their only goal is to make sure that there is always another goal beyond the goal that has been reached. In other words, the goal for NFs is to always have a goal. If NFs ever reach their goal without another goal beyond, despair and depression often result.

NF adults love seminars, workshops, continuing education classes, or simply any kind of educational class that sounds interesting. They are on an endless search to find out who they really are. And this search is no ordinary search. It must have meaning. Meaning and significance are always at the center of what their life is all about.

Much of what NFs enjoy about their endless search for understanding and meaning are the people they meet along the way. They thrive on interaction with others. When they approach the subject of relationships, they are often very idealistic, both offering more of themselves than they can give and expecting more of others than can be given.

NFs' expectations are often expressed through writing. Most writers are NFs (including this author). They, both male and female, are also drawn to professions in which they can work with other people. The ministry, counseling, and teaching are strong attractions to NFs. They also make great salespeople, selling on the basis of their warm personalities. Public relations and advertising also attract a high percentage of NFs.

Procedures are peripheral to NFs. If our SJ coworker, who wrote the *Standard Operating Procedures* manual, gives it to an NF, the NF's first response might be to rub the cover, then smell it, for NFs like to smell books. The NF might ask the SJ what it felt like to write a book. Several months later, the NF might ask about a certain procedure, and when told it was on page 14 in the *Standard Operating Procedures* manual, she might have to think a moment to remember where the manual is. Then she remembers that it is at home in the stack of books still unread on her nightstand. NFs love books and usually have a stack of them close by that they intend to read someday.

Whenever my wife and I give a seminar on this subject, the NFs in the audience are always the ones who are convinced that they are not only NFs, they are also SJs, SPs, and even NTs, if necessary. They truly feel they can be all four. Becoming each of these four temperaments can be part of their "becoming." But their curiosity about what it is like to be each of these four temperaments only proves that they are NFs!

Most self-help books are both written and read by NFs. They are always thinking about the possibilities, not only in themselves but also in people in general. They long to bring out the best in themselves and in everyone else. Life is defined best in terms of relationships. And for most NFs, life is a mission built around the search for understanding.

I hope these descriptions have helped confirm your choices of the four personality preferences you checked for yourself in the last chapter. If you were still undecided about any preference, the descriptions in this chapter should have helped to clear up your indecision.

Being in the middle between two preferences isn't necessarily a good thing, for it often indicates some degree of confusion. It can be likened to not knowing which hand is dominant. Do I write with my left hand or my right hand?

That would be a frustrating question if I had to ask it every time I had to write something. So before we move on to the next chapters, which will address the personalities of your children, look again at the descriptions in this chapter to see if any changes need to be made in the preferences you chose regarding your own personality.

CHAPTER FIVE

A Closer Look at the SP (Sensing/ Perceiving) Child

The Players and the Individualists

In chapter 1 we met four SPs: Rick and Sandy were the Extraverted SPs, whom we called the Players, and Ryan and Sarah were the Introverted SPs, whom we called the Individualists. Remember Rick, the one who was ready to play kickball even before the teams were chosen? And Sandy was the one who loved to perform. She knew how to keep everyone laughing. Ryan and Sarah were the quieter versions—Ryan followed Rick, enjoying kicking the ball while teams were chosen, and Sarah was the one who dressed "her way." The one theme that ran through each of their behaviors was a craving for action. SPs are active children beginning in infancy. From an early age, they love to move and hate to be confined. Playpens are like a prison to the SP toddler, restricting his or her desire for action.

As children, SPs are good eaters. They enjoy their food. They may be messy eaters, and they are usually the first ones to get dirty on a playground. You quickly learn to dress SPs last for church, for if they have to wait while others are still getting ready, they will instantly find a way to get dirty. If there is no dirt available, shirts will be untucked or hair ribbons will be dangling and desperately trying to at least stay in what had once been carefully combed hair. In the comic pages, Dennis the Menace is a classic Extraverted SP.

What Captures the SP Child's Attention

We've already noticed that activity captures SPs' attention. We can also capture their attention by recognizing what they are good at doing and by giving them the opportunity to demonstrate their skill. They are usually good at fixing things, so if something doesn't work and they want to work at fixing it, let them. Then have them tell you how they fixed it, for they usually will be able to fix it. Remember, SPs make great problem solvers, even when they're quite young.

A science teacher was trying to demonstrate electricity to her fifth-grade class. When a switch was flipped, a light was supposed to turn on but didn't. The teacher had new batteries and changed them around several times trying to make it work, but to no avail. The more she tried to make it work, the more she noticed Ryan starting to pay close attention to what was happening. Ryan, you'll remember, is an introverted SP, who often has difficulty paying attention in class. He's usually drawing in his notebook or looking longingly outside. Finally she asked, "Ryan, do you think you can fix this?"

With a big smile, Ryan walked up to the front of the classroom and took the apparatus over to the side. The teacher went on describing something else while Ryan tinkered first with the switch and then took apart the wiring and checked each contact. Within five minutes, he had it working again. The teacher wisely suggested that Ryan describe to the class how he had fixed the apparatus and why it now worked. After a moment's hesitation, Ryan excitedly launched into his description of what he had done. After the class, the teacher asked Ryan if he would like to go through the other science class sets of demonstration equipment and make sure each of them worked. That teacher got one SP's attention by letting him show what he could do by fixing something.

You may see in very young SP children a fascination with certain toys and the ability to play with them for hours. Simple toys are more fun than more complicated toys. For toddlers, emptying and refilling a kitchen cupboard over and over again will hold their attention for long periods of time. Then suddenly, they may lose interest and never pick up that toy or open that cupboard door again.

How SPs Handle Various Situations

School

Quite often, SP children are seen by the teacher as a control problem. They are often misunderstood since their need for movement and activity makes them disruptive. Scoldings and other forms of punishment are futile, for SPs seem indifferent to the teacher's frustrations. A look into SP children's desks or notebooks will be much like looking into their room at home. Everything appears to be a mess, but they know exactly where everything is and can find it when necessary.

Many times SPs are all too quickly diagnosed as either ADD (Attention Deficit Disorder) or ADHD (Attention Deficit Hyperactivity Disorder) due to their inability to sit very long, to pay attention, or to finish tasks on time. Before any child is diagnosed this way, both the parents and the school personnel need to understand what SP children are like in a classroom. I've talked with families whose child had been diagnosed as ADHD, but when that child was in workshop, in a drama class, or part of the school's football team, his ability to concentrate was amazing. Clearly what was misdiagnosed in this type of child as ADHD was but the misunderstood aspects of the SP temperament.

What needs to be understood is that SP children are not motivated by distant goals, such as grades at the end of the year or college choices eight years in the future. In fact, most of what the school and the classroom are about works in opposition to this type of child. It's not a matter of intelligence. SP children are constantly frustrated because in school they must stand in lines, wait for recess, and always be preparing for something that comes later, such as a test. All of these activities are usually meaningless to action-oriented SPs.

When school starts to become more theoretical and class subject matter becomes more abstract, SPs lose interest. The lecture method of teaching is the least effective way to teach SP children. Workbooks are considered worthless in their mind, for workbooks represent preparing, practicing, or rote-type learning, and SP children would rather just study the material and quickly take the test to get it over with.

SP children like to learn if you can make a game out of it or if you ask them to construct something. Contests that require a lot of activity are motivating to them. On the other hand, formal reports, showing how they arrived at an answer, or being forced to learn lots of detail, as in history class, seem like busywork to SP children. These are ways to shut down their motivation about school and learning. Homework is avoided by these children, if at all possible. And their avoidance of homework—or doing homework—usually doesn't affect their ability to perform on the test. SPs learn best by hands-on activities that challenge them, such as fixing the science class electricity experiment. They also enjoy learning through field trips, seeing films or other multimedia presentations, or interviewing other people.

Tasks
What is typical of SP children at school is also typical of them at home. They like to have full control over a task or they will lose interest. If you try to tell an SP child *how* to do something, he will quickly lose interest, for the fun of any task is figuring out how to do it. Even if you, as the parent, know the best way to do a task, allow the SP child to figure out his own way of doing it. You might learn something. Of course, if he does something one way today, it most certainly means that tomorrow he will try to accomplish the same thing a different way.

SPs are very literal children. They take you at your word. This can be very frustrating for a parent, for SPs are masters at separating the exact "letter of the law" from the "spirit of the law." Cynthia Tobias[3] tells this story of a girl who was an SP:

> In elementary school, this girl's teacher was passing around a pussy willow so everyone could touch and play with it. The teacher issued a strong warning that, *whatever* they did, they were not to put the pussy willow in their ears. This SP girl was the last one to

3 Cynthia Tobias, *The Way They Learn* (Colorado Springs, Colo.: Focus on the Family Publishing, 1984), 66–67.

get the pussy willow. While waiting for her turn, she drove herself crazy wondering *why* the teacher had warned them about putting the pussy willow in their ears. When the pussy willow finally got to her, she "scrunched down in her seat, hid her face, and stuck it not in her ear but in her nose! It went in easy, but it got stuck coming out." She got punished by the teacher for her little scientific experiment. To this day she insists she had not disobeyed the teacher. She had not put the pussy willow in her *ear!*

Parents may experience this same literalness when they tell their SP child to stop jumping on his bed. Later, when punishing that same SP child for jumping on his sister's bed, the parents have a difficult time seeing that the SP's literal interpretation of the parents' demand was that he not jump on *his* bed—nothing was ever said about *his sister's* bed.

SP children's rooms are usually in various states of messiness. Of course, to them the room is not dirty or messy—it's just the way they want it. They are usually much too busy to have to "reorganize" their room in order to meet with the parents' irrelevant demand that it be different than it is. Not only is their room a collection of various "important" things, their pockets are often filled with stuff they just might need while playing.

For these children, the *process* of any task is what is important. That's often why cleaning their room is so irrelevant. They are not interested in the finished product—a clean room. They are looking only at the process, and why should they participate in the process of cleaning a room when there are so many other fun things to do? A wise parent makes a game out of cleaning a room or offers some special activity as a reward for when the cleaning is finished.

Of course, most of the time when SP children do clean their room, one of two things happens. Either they become absorbed in some toy or other fascinating item and start playing with it instead of cleaning, or they quickly push things out of sight—into drawers, under the bed, or behind the closet door. Again, their response will be literal. You said, "Clean your room," not "Clean out your drawers" or "Clean out under your bed" or "Straighten your closet."

Family and holidays

Family events and holidays can be a problem to SP children, especially as they get older. If parents want to do the same things over and over again each year "as a tradition," their SP child will get restless and look for ways to throw a monkey wrench into the plans. He doesn't do this because he's a bad kid; it's just that he can't stand routine and predictability. SP children's love of variety and spontaneity means that they don't like to plan too far ahead. This doesn't mean, however, that they don't want to know until the last minute. This may work when they are younger, but as they hit their teens, their spontaneity often involves hanging around with friends. Then they need to be informed well in advance, even though they will hassle you about going right up until you leave together for the event.

Since most family events are controlled by the parents, which gives SPs a sense of being manipulated—something they want to avoid as much as possible—it helps to involve them in planning the day or event. This will give them some sense of controlling their own activity. Their suggestions may be wild and even inappropriate for the intent of the event, but who knows, their creative energy may produce some good ideas you never would have considered. If they are left out of the planning or get too bored, they will probably act out and create a crisis of some type. That's how SPs get a reputation for being troublemakers; it's their only response to boredom.

Discipline

This is a real problem area for parents of an SP child, partly because it seems that these children are always getting into messes or causing some kind of trouble. Their sense of fun can be very impulsive and therefore is not always appropriate, so they often say things they don't really mean and do things they haven't really thought through. If their mouth has gotten them into trouble with you, it might be helpful to ask them if that's really what they meant to say. The momentary reflection caused by that question may lead SPs to take back their words. Parents are wise in giving their SP child this "out," for often what was said was done so impulsively, especially if the child is an Extraverted SP, who often speaks before thinking.

To SP children, rules are guidelines, not absolutes. They think quickly on their feet, so when caught breaking what parents consider the absolute rule, they are good at talking their way out of trouble. They may do this by pointing out all the previous exceptions the parents have made in not consistently applying this rule, either to them or to siblings.

Spankings are a waste of time with SP children, as are any other forms of ultimatum. If an SP's parents use spanking as a means of discipline, they may find themselves spanking a little stoic who is doing everything in his power not to cry. When the spanking is over, he will look at you and ask, "Are you done? Now can I go back out and play?"

Because of this indifference to verbal or physical punishment, most SP children would be considered "strong-willed."

If you follow Dennis the Menace in the comics, you remember that the form of punishment that works best with SP children is to sit them in a chair, facing the corner. The most horrible form of punishment for them is to be removed from life's stimuli. Send SPs to their room as punishment, and they will find something to play with. Ground them and they will drive you crazy with their restlessness.

The best way to discipline SP children is to work out with them in advance the consequences of any misbehavior. If they can have input regarding the rules and the consequences for breaking those rules, they will better understand the purpose of the discipline and may be even more consistent and fair than the parent in imposing those consequences when the rule is broken. SPs expect and want parents to be the authority, but they want to have some input into the process of how that authority is exercised.

Often, SP children will misbehave because they are overstimulated. Their drive for action and spontaneity has them so worked up that they don't know how to stop. One of the main purposes of discipline with these children is to help train them in how to control themselves and how to relax. In addition, concentration skills need to be taught, and they need to learn to delay gratification.

Responsibility

Setting up consequences prior to misbehavior is a good way to teach SPs responsibility. Giving them pets to care for is another good way. Typically, SPs love animals. They may play too roughly with an animal at times, so parents must teach responsibility by helping them know what is appropriate play with the animal. Making SP children responsible for the care of the animal is also an important way for them to learn responsibility. Remember that duty and responsibility are *secondary* issues to the SP child; action is what rules.

You can also reinforce responsible behavior in SP children by focusing on performing the task, not the outcome of a task. To say to SPs, "Hey, great! You won!" is not a meaningful statement. Saying, "You played well" is meaningful. So to say to SPs, "Has the dog been fed?" is not going to be as effective as saying, "I really appreciate your caring about the dog and making sure he gets fed." Contrary to what some might say, for SP children, you need to praise the performance, not the outcome.

Parents need to begin to teach responsibility early with SP children. Their love of action coupled with their impulsivity needs to be contained within a growing sense of responsibility. Helping them see the consequences of their behavior, especially as it affects other people in the family, will need to be repeated often. If you are a regular reader of "Dennis the Menace," you know he still hasn't made a connection between his behavior and Mr. Wilson's bad moods.

Relationships

Extraverted SP children are going to have lots of friends, especially compared with Introverted SP children. But both types of SP children will organize their friendships around their activities. During soccer season, their friends will be on the soccer team. During school, their friends will be the ones they play with on the playground. On Sundays their friends will be the church kids. In other words, SP children, especially Extraverted SPs, will be gregarious in making friends through their activities, but the friendships will be associated with an activity. When they are no longer involved in that activity and begin a new one, their friends will be part of the new activity.

If SPs stay with an activity over several years, they can develop long friendships with those who share that activity with them. It is important that parents encourage the maintenance of friendships when the activity stops so there can be some continuity with friends over the years.

SOURCES OF STRESS IN THE SP CHILD

As you can see from the topics already discussed, the major source of stress for SP children is going to be too many rules and restrictions. While it may seem to parents of such a child that they need to "clamp down" on him, that is the exact opposite of what really needs to be done. The more parents can lighten up without letting go of either the child or the issue, the better off the child and the family will be. It is also important for the parent of an SP child to learn how to differentiate between major and minor issues, learning how to let go of the minor ones.

Trying to force SP children into a rigid schedule will only frustrate them and make their behavior even worse. If you can find ways to not force an issue with them, you will get much further than with an ultimatum. SPs will resist arbitrary ultimatums with everything they have within them, even if it causes them pain in the process. Keeping options open is a way of life for SP children, so stress builds when options are taken away or limited.

SPECIAL PARENTING TASKS WITH AN SP CHILD

Obviously, it takes a lot of patience and a lot of energy to parent SP children. As with Dennis the Menace, it also requires other people to be in the process. Even though Mr. Wilson doesn't appear to enjoy Dennis, he and his wife provide a lot of help to Dennis's parents. All parents of an SP child need a Mr. and Mrs. Wilson in their life to give them a break.

The key parenting skill that seems to be needed with SP children is an ability to keep them active. Too much downtime for SPs can lead to boredom, which leads to the wrong kinds of actions. Knowing when to take a break to get your own parental batteries recharged can help a lot. The other skill needed is the ability to create choices for them. If they feel that they are being forced into a mold or routine, they will resist. But if they are given choices, they can and will make good choices.

Discipline will always be a challenge for the parents of an SP child. One of the best ways to discipline these children is through logical consequences. Give them a clear warning prior to a problem that when certain misbehaviors take place, certain consequences will also take place. Then, when the misbehavior takes place, parents can very matter-of-factly inform their child that because he chose to behave that way, he must now suffer the consequence. If these conditions are worked out in advance with SP children—and make sense to them—it is often the only type of discipline that will work with them.

THE EXTRAVERTED SP AND THE INTROVERTED SP

When we looked at Rick and Sandy on the playground, we could see a marked difference between them and Ryan and Sarah. This is the difference between the Introverted SP (Ryan and Sarah) and the Extraverted SP (Rick and Sandy). But with the SP child, the main difference between the Extravert and the Introvert will be what we see on the surface, not what goes on inside. Everything that is true of the Extravert is also true of the Introvert. You just can't see it so clearly in the Introverted SP, whereas the Extraverted SP will make certain you see it.

Both are full of fun. They keep a family laughing. They have a passionate enjoyment of life that is contagious, and in a way, they epitomize everything we think of when we think of a happy child. They will give parents gray hairs with their risk taking, but they always seem to have a knack for landing on their feet. As adults and parents, we can learn a lot about enjoying life from watching our SP children.

SUMMARY
Remember, the SP child

- is active
- is a good eater
- can always find the mud puddle
- loves activities
- can be a problem to the teacher in school
- is often mistaken for an ADHD child
- is not motivated by distant goals
- is challenged by practical, hands-on experience
- is very literal
- tolerates well a general sense of "messiness"
- loves the process much more than the finished product
- sees rules as guidelines, not absolutes
- isn't impressed by spankings
- can easily be overstimulated
- doesn't come naturally to a sense of responsibility
- therefore needs to be taught responsibility
- can best learn responsibility through consequences
- makes friends through shared activities
- will always be a challenge to parents
- always adds fun and life to the family

CHAPTER SIX

A Closer Look at the SJ (Sensing/ Judging) Child

The Organizers and the Monitors

In chapter 1 we met four SJs: Brad and Margaret were the Extraverted SJs whom we identified as the Organizers on the playground. Brad organized the kickball game, and Margaret organized the hopscotch game. Bill and Miriam were the Introverted SJs, whom we identified as the Monitors. They were always aware of what needed to be done, even though they deferred to Brad and Margaret. But if necessary, duty would have called, and they would have organized the games just as effectively as Brad or Margaret.

The one theme that runs through every SJ is a need for stability. They thrive when they know that what is true today is also going to be true tomorrow. SJ children are very vulnerable to changes in their routines. Even such a thing as moving can be very unsettling to this type of child. They like to live in the same house, have the same friends, go to the same school, and attend the same church, for this sense of sameness gives

SJs a feeling of security. They are especially vulnerable to family instability and are often the most devastated when their parents bicker a lot or when they separate or divorce. As infants, SJs are usually very compliant babies, seeking from a very early age to please. As they get to be toddlers, their need to please causes them to begin early to take care of others. They are the ones in nursery school who are likely to tell the teacher that Johnny wet his pants or that Megan isn't sharing her toys. It isn't that they are natural-born tattletales; they are just being helpful. In the comic pages, Margaret, Dennis the Menace's friend, is a typical SJ. She always seems to know the right thing to do and spends a lot of time and energy trying to get Dennis (the SP child) to shape up.

What Captures the SJ Child's Attention

If activity captures the attention of SP children, appreciation and approval capture the attention of SJ children. Put a smiley face on one of their school papers, and they will take great pride in this proof of the teacher's approval. You've made their day! If a parent praises an SJ child for a job well done, she will usually ask if there is anything else that needs to be done. SJs are the only one of the four temperaments that will actively seek rewards simply for the sake of the recognition. The objective is to get the smiley face on the paper or the gold star on the chart. In some cases, the prize itself is almost anticlimactic in that *earning* the reward is so satisfying to them.

If we were to visit Margaret's house, we would probably notice her "reward" chart on the refrigerator. Margaret would explain to us how she gets the gold stars and how many stars she needs to earn in order to get the prize she is working toward.

SP children will work for gold stars if and when it suits

them. NT children view gold stars as meaningless, and to NFs, earning gold stars seems cold and impersonal. Only SJ children will work the chart consistently. They may even save their charts, just as they save their smiley-faced papers and treasure the trophies or ribbons they have won. We talked with a group of SJ adults, and almost all of them still had schoolbooks, awards, and smiley-faced papers from elementary school.

How SJs Handle Various Situations

School

Our schools were made for SJ children. With more than two-thirds of the elementary teachers and administrators being SJs themselves, it is easy to see that schools were made by SJs for SJs. They do well in school, often because the values of the SJ teacher are shared by the SJ children. The highly structured classroom gives SJs a sense of security. It allows them to know what to do and when to do it. If a school has to change teachers in the middle of the year or if a teacher needs to make changes in the classroom, SJ children can become very unsettled.

SJ children study hard and are very responsible about being prepared. If they are to do an oral presentation in class, they will spend hours organizing and practicing what they are going to say. When they see other children simply "wing it" with their oral presentations, they are appalled at those children's irresponsibility.

If something isn't clear to SJ children about an assignment or about some procedure, they will ask the teacher for clarification. Their questions often seem nitpicky to the other types of children, but they are important questions for SJs. Knowing how to do something can often be even more important than what they are actually supposed to do. It is extremely important to them that they do things correctly.

Usually SJ children adjust well to school, although the Introverted SJs may appear shy at first. They love to please the teacher, so they do not usually ask the why questions because questioning anything is sometimes seen as challenging the teacher's authority. As they progress through the grades, it is often the SJs who run for student body offices or who enjoy being the hall monitors or filling just about any other jobs that allow them to be helpful to the teacher and the administrator alike.

The lecture method of teaching is very satisfying for SJ children, especially if the lecture is organized so that note taking can be done easily. They love workbooks, for workbooks help them prepare for the next day's lesson. They enjoy a number of subjects including math, spelling, reading, history, geography, and science. In high school and college they will probably gravitate toward business classes or study to become teachers themselves. They usually aren't as interested in subjects such as debating, drama, or English literature.

SJs have strong study habits. Homework is taken very seriously. They like to drill and memorize before a test. They are into sequential learning tasks, and they feel good when they can see how what they learned last week is helping them learn something new this week. Their notebooks are neatly organized, and from the early grades they are meticulous about their assignment book. They like to plan their work carefully and have a clear schedule of when things are due. When they do get stuck, they need someone to patiently show them, step-by-step, what they need to do.

Sometimes SJ children will take an assignment too

literally, not thinking that the words in the assignment may be an abstraction. For instance, an SJ child being asked to list the natural resources of a region in a geography class may have difficulty doing this because the book doesn't say "These are the natural resources of. . . ." Here again, a little step-by-step help will help break through their literalness and allow them to see what is expected. They work well with time limits and are able to pace themselves so they aren't too pushed at the deadline.

What is difficult for SJs in school is participating in a group activity. Often in a group, the teacher's instructions may appear to be unclear. As a result, the SJs will spend time in the beginning working out procedural rules for the group activity so everyone clearly knows what to do.

Tasks

SJs approach tasks with a focus on the finished product. If it's a game or a sports activity, they want to hear from the parents, "Hey, you won! Isn't that great!" They aren't concerned about or even aware sometimes of the effort they made in the process that got them there. The same is true of tasks around the house. SJ children love routines in the home and so welcome a list of chores they may be expected to do. To them, it isn't the fun or the experience of doing something that is important. They will work hard simply to get your approval and feedback. To SJs, any task becomes a means to the end, which is to get approval.

Doing crafts with a parent can be very enjoyable for SJ children, and their interest in crafts will often continue to be enjoyable for them as adults. Working with Dad in his workshop or learning to sew with Mom are special events in the life of an SJ child. But more important than learning how is the joy of actually creating something. So when SJs can make something in Dad's workshop or actually sew a dress or shirt, they are hooked. It is a special treat to receive a gift of something an SJ child has made, for you know it comes from the heart.

The SJ child's room is going to be quite different from the SP's room. It is usually neat and orderly, not only on the surface, but in the drawers and closet as well. The SJs' natural attention to detail means that they like everything in its place. And this behavior can become routine if parents are careful to make sure they praise their SJ on a regular basis or give her a gold star on her chart for keeping her room neat.

Family and holidays

Holidays are especially important to SJ children, for these holidays represent family traditions. SJs enjoy being with the family, and holidays often allow them to be with the extended family. When the family has attached strong traditions to these holidays, SJs will celebrate with abandon. They enjoy listening to stories about the family history and will often ask questions that keep the storyteller talking.

When decorating for the holidays, SJs want to help. They want to know where everything goes, perhaps having an even better memory of "how it was last year" than does the parent. They may suggest that you take a photograph of this year's decorations so you can duplicate them next year. They want to learn how to cook the special holiday recipes and want to help you cook them. SJ children not only remember how the holiday was celebrated last year, they resist any changes. The only change allowed can be an additional decoration or an additional menu item—or an additional tradition. Knowing that the family will celebrate birthdays and holidays the same way each year gives SJs a sense of security.

Discipline

SJ children are usually very receptive to discipline. They respond quickly to scoldings, criticism, and even spankings. But harsh discipline is usually quite unnecessary for them since part of their makeup is the desire to please the parents. Often the mere threat of punishment is enough to bring their behavior back into line.

Since SJs are very behaviorally oriented, the reward system of putting gold stars on a chart, as we've already noted, works very well as a motivator of good behavior. Obviously, any form of discipline with them needs to be clearly spelled out in advance, with the rules uniformly applied to each child in the family. SJ children have a strong respect for authority and expect parents to act with firmness and fairness. Being right or wrong is also important to SJs, so if they insist that something is unfair or that something is being wrongly interpreted by a parent, it would be good for the parent to stop and discuss with them the point they are trying to make.

Responsibility

Being responsible is where SJ children shine. It is part of what makes them tick. Dependability and duty are high priorities for SJs. In fact, they take responsibility so seriously that negative criticism or comments can actually motivate them to do better, whereas negative criticism is more likely to demotivate other personality types.

SJ children also respond well to authority. If a teacher says something, it must be true. If the principal says something, then it's even more true. Other authority figures in their lives have a strong influence on them as well. The pastor, the Sunday school teacher, the Cub Scout leader— all of these people are authorities, and what they say to an SJ child is of the utmost importance.

If anything, SJ children will tend to be too responsible, trying to please as many people as possible. They take on more than they can do and then overwork themselves in order to do it all. Whenever you see an SJ child begin to act irresponsibly, something is wrong. She may be sick or so discouraged that she can no longer motivate herself. Helping SJ children become more aware of their limitations early in their life will not only help them develop more realistic expectations for themselves, it will also serve them well when they become adults.

Relationships

The relationship style of SJ children is what might be called traditional. They relate to others the way we all think we are "supposed" to relate. They are caring and concerned about others and want the best for everyone. But other temperaments don't always see SJ children as caring. Instead, they are often seen by others as parental. Out of their sense of caring and responsibility, they are likely to act like the teacher or the parent to their friends.

Sometimes this concern for others leads them to worry about the slightest little thing that might go wrong in a relationship. Their tendency to worry, which can be seen even at a very early age, often goes along with their natural attention to detail, which was mentioned earlier. That, along with the SJs' natural pessimism, need for approval, and strong drive to take care of others, makes worrying a strong part of their personality. Quite often, these worries will take the form of a stomachache or some other physical ailment.

SOURCES OF STRESS FOR THE SJ CHILD

As you may already sense, one of the biggest sources of stress for SJs is having too much to do. The desire to be responsible coupled with the drive for approval makes it very hard for them to say no to anyone. The sense of being overwhelmed can often begin at a very young age for SJs and continue on into adulthood. Parents need to help their SJ child understand that it is sometimes OK to say no. Usually this is a lesson SJs must learn from the example of the parents, not just from words. At least one parent probably has the SJ temperament as well, and that parent will struggle with the same tendency to try to do too much. Both need to learn that saying no is a healthy skill to develop.

It is also very stressful to SJ children if they do not have enough advance notice about some task or event so they can prepare themselves. Finding out about something at the last minute, especially when they could have been told earlier, makes them feel uncomfortable and is not easily accepted by SJs. In addition, situations in which others' expectations are not clear are also unsettling to SJs, giving them a feeling of insecurity and uncertainty.

SPECIAL PARENTING TASKS WITH AN SJ CHILD

Parenting SJ children is usually a pleasure since those children are motivated to please the parents. As a result, when expectations are clearly stated, rules are not complicated, life is consistent, and other family members know how to be specific and literal in their communication, SJs thrive.

On the other hand, whenever there is tension in the home, SJ children know and feel it, no matter how hard the parents try to hide the problems. If the parents are not getting along or are talking of separation or divorce, SJ children are especially at risk. If this happens, they will need a lot of reassurance and will need the support of the extended family in order to feel a sense of stability and continuity. Adaptability is not their forte in life; responsibility is.

THE EXTRAVERTED SJ AND THE INTROVERTED SJ

Back on the playground, when we compare Brad and Margaret with Bill and Miriam, the basic difference will be that the Introverted SJs are going to be a "quieter" version of the Extraverted SJs. Or we might see Introverted SJs as somewhat slower than the Extraverted SJs in actively taking charge in a situation. Many of their traits, such as responsibility, response to approval, and the need for consistency will be equally apparent. What appears to be shyness but is in reality only a sense of quietness will be the only obvious difference.

IN SUMMARY
Remember, the SJ child

- is easily captured by approval and appreciation
- loves charts with gold stars or smiley faces
- thrives in the elementary and secondary school environment
- loves to be prepared
- enjoys a good lecture in class
- enjoys the finished product much more than the process of getting there
- keeps her room neat
- loves family holidays because she loves traditions
- is very responsive to discipline, so there is no need to overdo it; will respond even to the threat of discipline
- regards responsibility and duty as favorite concepts
- cares a lot about friends but can be parental to them

- may take on too much to do and then be stressed out and overwhelmed
- likes to plan ahead; doesn't really like last-minute surprises
- likes to please the parent
- can be overly sensitive to disruption and tension in the home

CHAPTER SEVEN

A Closer Look at the NT (iNtuitive/ Thinking) Child

The Competitors and the Explorers
In chapter 1 we met four NTs. Calvin and Abbey were the Extraverted NTs, whom we called the Competitors. They liked to organize things also but were very concerned that things be fair and that everyone take matters seriously. Competition was the name of the game on the playground. Carl and Annie were the Introverted NTs, whom we called the Explorers. They acted as though they lived in their own world, which might include a spontaneous study of bugs under a rock.

The one theme that runs through each of these four personalities is what has been called a "curiosity lust." From an early age, their favorite question is "Why?" They might ask, "Why does the sun come up here instead of over there?" or "Why does the light go on over there when I move the switch over here?" Another way they ask this question is "What would happen if . . .?" For example, they wonder what would happen if they put their toast in their milk or what would happen if they put salt in the pepper shaker and pepper in the saltshaker. It is important that parents understand that these questions are not asked in order to annoy them. NT children genuinely want to know about and understand as much of the universe as possible.

This thirst for knowledge leads many NT children to learn to talk and read early. These early abilities often lead others to see NT children as being very precocious. In fact, NTs can be frustrated at a very early age because they believe they should already know how to read. They love to read and be read to by others, and they will want to continue being read to long after the other types of children have lost interest.

As infants, NT children can often appear to be rather solemn. They take life seriously from the start and early on seem intent on improving themselves. They can become very frustrated with themselves if they don't do something as well as they think they should be able to do it.

WHAT CAPTURES THE NT CHILD'S ATTENTION

So far, we've seen that SP children are motivated and energized by activity and SJ children by responsibility and duty. NT children are motivated and energized by the mysteries of the unknown. They want to be able to understand, explain, predict, and control the realities around them. So life becomes an adventure of exploration and research.

This can be seen in the little NT child who is deeply involved in a new toy. He is not really playing with the toy as much as he is experimenting with it. As you watch him, you'll notice that he does not play with the toy in the way it was designed to be played with, at least not for very long.

Soon he experiments with the toy to see what else he might be able to do with it.

Once NT children understand a toy, they will become bored with it. This often leads parents to give their NT child toys that are meant for older children, which is not appropriate. Parents need to understand that age-appropriate toys that are complex are the best toys for NT children, for the complexity gives them a lot to explore and to attempt to understand.

For example, a friend's NT preschooler loves Lego blocks. He has a vast collection of them, and he is able to endlessly create different things out of his blocks. He is so into his Lego blocks that he often sneaks them into his bed so he can continue to create things even after the light has been turned off.

HOW NTS HANDLE VARIOUS SITUATIONS

School

NT children usually do quite well in school. They focus more on their studies than on social or recreational activities. They are in school to learn, and learning is what life is all about for them. Introverted NT children are often loners in school. Many times they feel that they are truly alone and that no one really understands them. Since NTs make up about 12 percent of the population, that means that in a class of thirty-two children, approximately four children will be NTs, and only one of those four children will be an Introverted NT. So often an Introverted NT child *is* the only one in a classroom who sees life as he does.

What we've noticed with NT children over the years is that they are either overachievers or underachievers, seldom in between. Those who are overachievers have been able to figure out the system of the school and of the teacher and make it work for themselves. Or they have enlisted an SJ friend to help them study and not miss the details. Those who are underachievers are usually bored with the methodical, step-by-step process of traditional classroom instruction. NTs may sit in class daydreaming instead of paying attention to the teacher. They may even fail a class they don't like (which usually means that they find the class or the teacher very boring), while getting an A in another class where the teacher has found a way to stimulate their curiosity and keep their attention focused. This is usually more true of Introverted NT children but will also be true at times of Extraverted NTs.

Older NT children will enjoy a lecture as long as it is prepared well and presented well. They will consider the lecture to be done well if it is concise, contains accurate information, and avoids—at all costs—any repetition. Statements must stand on their own, so if NTs believe the teacher is wrong about something, they will question the teacher's position. Their willingness to challenge the teacher, as well as their love of debate, might make them appear arrogant, but this is typical NT behavior. Whereas SJs will accept the word of the teacher, NTs will take a stand on principle if they think the teacher is wrong or inaccurate.

In the early grades especially, NT children can be very perfectionistic, especially about their own performance and grades. Their perfectionism may also mean that they take more time than expected to finish a project to their satisfaction. This can be frustrating to a parent who wants to say, "It's good enough; just turn it in." What the parent considers to be "good enough" may be far short of an NT child's standards for the quality of his work. In fact, NTs can be so concerned about the quality of their work that they will seldom, if ever, turn in an unfinished assignment.

NT children are basically independent learners, regardless of whether they are Extraverts or Introverts. They thrive on independent projects. They don't like to work on group projects, for others usually do not share their high standards for the quality of their work. NTs also do not appreciate group discussions, usually choosing not to participate.

Extraverted NT children are often placed in leadership positions beginning in the early grades. NTs are born leaders and in some cases could be described as being unable *not* to be leaders. They can be seen on the playground organizing events and games. In the classroom, they sometimes compete with the teacher in suggesting how to better organize the room. When class officers are elected, they are the innovative campaigners who will run against the traditional SJs for class president. Usually it will be the NTs who win for president and the SJs who will become the secretaries and treasurers of the class.

Tasks

NT children will approach tasks in much the same way they approach a school assignment. "Let me do it myself" is their motto. Watching their NT child do something routine can be very exasperating for parents, for NTs will want to study how the task can be done more efficiently, and parents just want the task finished. For example, if the task is to feed the dog, an NT child may spend hours figuring out a way to automatically measure out how much dog food is needed and then set up a timer that automatically releases the right amount into the bowl at the right time. He is a little scientist and inventor, often coming up with intricate ways to do a simple task more efficiently.

Chores have to be fit into all the other activities NT children are involved in. Introverted NTs can often get lost in a project, skipping meals and forgetting to go to bed, unless parents insist and remind them. Our NT son spent hours as a twelve- and thirteen-year-old working on building his own computer with parts he collected from various sources. This was back in the early seventies, when large personal computers were first becoming available. When he got his computer working, he had also mastered in his own mind much of the theory on how a computer actually works. The fact that he had boxes of leftover parts didn't bother him at all; it only meant that he now had a collection of spare computer parts. And doing his chores during this time was an unwelcome interruption, especially if we demanded they be done at a specific time. We had to learn to be flexible in our expectations.

Often NT children are rather erratic in the way they keep their rooms. While it may be neat on the surface, check in the drawers or in the closet and you'll often find messes or extensive collections of all kinds stuffed here and there. There may be a rock collection in one place, while a collection of items to be examined under the microscope fills another drawer. Rather than being neat, the NT's room could better be described as efficient. For NTs, aesthetics always takes a backseat to efficiency.

Family and holidays

Family rituals and holiday celebrations are not a very appealing part of life for NT children. Tradition is not valued for its own sake. If there is a tradition, there must be some meaning to it. To say that this is the way we have always done something means nothing to NTs. If you've gone to Grandma's every Christmas, your NT child will still ask, "But why do we have to go this year?" Your answer needs to be logically thought through if it has any chance of being accepted by your NT child. His "but why . . .?" is not just a game; it is a serious question that he wants you to take seriously.

On the other hand, NTs are very loyal to the family. If the importance of a tradition or a celebration can be explained to them in terms of its importance to the family as a whole, they will usually join in and enjoy themselves.

Discipline

When it comes to parenting NT children, parents are almost irrelevant. Most NT children raise themselves. Discipline is usually unnecessary, for NTs work hard at self-correction. Their internal standards of improvement lead them to be very self-critical, which forms the basis of their self-correcting behaviors.

Physical punishment is experienced as a deep violation by NTs and is really unnecessary. We were speaking about this to a group of missionaries, and one young man who was an NT said, "Why didn't you tell my mother that?" He went on to say that every time his mother spanked him when he was a little boy, he had thought to himself, *This is so unnecessary! I have already taken care of the problem!* In the same way, verbal reprimands or criticism by a parent are humiliating and devastating to NTs. They may appear indifferent at the time, but they are usually deeply hurt by such criticism—because, on the inside, they have already corrected themselves.

Because of this self-correcting behavior, NT children will usually be obedient and compliant. However, if a parent becomes overbearing or overly intrusive on an issue that matters to an NT child, he will often stand his ground and logically argue with the parent on the merits, or lack of merits, related to what the parent wants. If it comes to a choice between accepting authority or standing on a principle, NT children will always choose to stand on the principle, regardless of who represents the authority. When this happens, it is wise to slow down the process and listen to their arguments and then reason logically with them so they can understand the basis of your position.

Responsibility

The way NT children approach responsibility is through the search for competency. They will usually be most responsible in the area of learning, choosing to take the difficult subjects in school and working hard to do well. When they encounter incompetency, whether in a teacher, a coach, or anyone else in authority, NTs may act irresponsibly by withdrawing internally and going off somewhere else in their mind. A classic example of this is seen the comic strip "Calvin and Hobbes," in which Calvin is often found sitting in school, but in his mind he is exploring outer space and fighting aliens. If NTs encounter boredom early on in school, they may become underachievers, choosing instead to follow in Calvin's steps and explore undiscovered worlds in the privacy of their mind.

Relationships

Relationships are difficult for NT children, especially for the Introverted NTs. In many ways they are socially inept. Manners are a mystery to them, mostly because they don't understand any logical reason for keeping elbows off the table or placing a napkin in their lap. Because of this, NTs are often misunderstood. The stereotypical nerd is usually an Introverted NT.

Since NT children respond very well to coaching and to feedback regarding the quality of what they are doing, they can be—and need to be—trained in social skills and how to relate to others. Parents need to patiently help NT children understand how their behavior affects the feelings of another person. Tact and empathy need to be taught, beginning at an early age. If social skills can be put in a context where NTs are challenged to become competent, they will not only learn these social skills but can excel at them. But to do this, parents need to seriously answer the why questions surrounding the whole area of social relationships. One way to do this is to stimulate the intellectual curiosity of NTs regarding manners or social behaviors. You could make this a topic of study and research. Have them look up manners on the Internet or study how other cultures define manners. You can also challenge them to analyze with you another person's response to their behavior. Or you might suggest that they research the history of manners; this could create children who are expert in understanding and defining manners. Frequent encouragement and praise for the *quality* of their efforts will aid in this task.

SOURCES OF STRESS FOR THE NT CHILD

Perhaps the greatest source of stress for NT children is what happens when a parent or other adult gets tired of the why questions. This is especially true for some of the harder why questions, which are usually very important to NTs. Another important stressor for NTs is having someone who isn't competent *pretend* to know the answers. They would much rather the adult just admit, "I don't know."

If SJ children get stressed by having too much to do, NT children get stressed by having too much to learn. Their love for learning and their desire to share with everyone what they are learning can know no limits. The parents of NT children need to help them learn how to set priorities and to face the reality that they can't learn everything.

NT children also struggle with learning something or dealing with something thoroughly. They learn best by hitting the highlights—getting the overall picture. Being forced to delve deeply into the details about a subject can be very frustrating for them. On the other hand, since NTs don't realize that they are only hitting the highlights, they sometimes need help in seeing the parts they might have missed. This will help them avoid the stress caused by finding this out too late in a situation.

Unreasonable deadlines are also very stressful for NTs. They can't stand to be rushed, for this only serves to raise their anxiety that they are going to miss something important. Wise parents can help by giving them the time they need, knowing that children and young people can recover rather quickly from a short night's sleep and knowing that NTs would rather have less sleep one night so they can finish something their way than be rushed to finish just because parents said they must.

SPECIAL PARENTING TASKS AN NT CHILD

One of the hardest things for parents of NT children to do is to believe that they will truly self-correct. If your child is old enough, talk to him about the way you typically discipline and about ways you can work together in helping him with his own self-discipline. Along this same line, you will need to help your NT child not be so self-critical. This could be a major problem for NT children and can seriously lower their self-esteem. Understanding God's grace and acceptance of themselves can be an important part of their acceptance of themselves.

Typically, parents work hard at teaching their NT daughters important social skills, along with an understanding of their emotional makeup. It is equally important that parents teach these same lessons to their NT sons. Ways to do this are outlined in chapter 9.

THE EXTRAVERTED NT AND THE INTROVERTED NT

Because both the male and female Introverted NT children have rich inner lives, it is especially important that parents stay connected with their children. This cannot be done by pressuring children to spend time with the family or with a parent. It can be done by recognizing NT children's need for solitude and setting up ways for the parent to support that need. For example, a parent can talk with the Introverted NT child about this need and ask him when the need is most pressing. Usually this will be after school, when the Introverted NT child is worn out by having to interact all day. Perhaps time for solitude can be set up between the child's arriving home from school and dinnertime. During this time, the Introverted NT child can be alone in his room, after, of course, saying hello to anyone at home. (And a quick hello is all that is expected.) After dinner the Introverted NT child can be expected to spend part of the evening with the family and part of it as he chooses. Recognizing his need for solitude gives him the opportunity to recognize his need for the family as well.

Extraverted NT children will often be out at the head of the pack. They are natural leaders, and leadership roles seem to fall into their lap. At times, parents of Extraverted NTs will wonder who the parent really is, for Extraverted NT children will be very obvious about their competency, sometimes to the point that the parents wonder what their role is in the child-rearing process!

Again, it is important that the parents of an Extraverted NT remain the parents—and stay involved with the child. Rather than retreating to his room as the Introverted NT child did, the Extravert will be out and about making things happen. Even in kindergarten, the Extraverted NT will be trying to organize the playground, probably unaware of that vague internal sense that he knows how to do it better.

IN SUMMARY
Remember, the NT child

- has a lust for knowledge
- loves why questions
- loves the "What would happen if . . . ?" possibilities
- loves to explore the unknown
- would rather understand a toy than play with it
- often does well in school as long as he isn't bored by lengthy explanations
- often challenges a teacher if he thinks the teacher is wrong
- learns best independently
- can be a perfectionist
- gravitates naturally to leadership roles
- can get lost in his many projects, even forgetting to eat
- loves to collect things
- always looks for the meaning in things, including holiday celebrations
- tends to raise himself, making discipline almost irrelevant
- finds physical punishment a deep violation of his person
- finds responsibility through his drive toward competency
- has difficulty in relationships, especially if he is an Introvert
- becomes very upset over anything considered "unreasonable"

CHAPTER EIGHT

A Closer Look at the NF (iNtuitive/ Feeling) Child

The Relators and the Dreamers
The last four characters we met in chapter 1 were NF children. Julie and Daren were the Extraverted NFs, whom we called the Relators, and Jennifer and Dan were the Introverted NFs, the Dreamers. The one theme that ran through each of their behaviors was the centrality of relationships. From a very early age, the NF child is seen by others as charming, and she draws others to her. Whereas NT children need to be taught social skills, NF children are naturally social, seeming to understand innately how to get along with others from an early age.

NF children often talk early, and it may seem that Extraverted NFs never stop talking. When their ability to talk is coupled with their vivid imagination, they can make up stories that are very intricate and convincing.

One little NF boy was very sad one day in nursery school. When the teacher commented on how sad he was, he explained that his best friend's mother had just died. He went on to fill in the details of his story, explaining how his friend was sad and that family members were all coming to the house, etc. Only when the mother of the NF child picked him up from nursery school and the teacher expressed her sympathy for his friend's mother did the teacher find out that everything she had been told existed only in this child's imagination.

Obviously, it can be very difficult for young NFs to separate imagination from telling lies. Wise parents will be aware of the use of the imagination in concocting these stories and will help their NF children understand the importance of separating imagination from the truth.

One can also see the uniqueness of NF children by the way they play with toys. NT children want to analyze and understand a toy. SP children need toys that can be manipulated. SJ children simply want a toy to play with. NF children want toys that can spark their imagination. To them, a toy is a fantasy object. They often weave fantasy stories around each of their toys, including stuffed animals, cars, dolls, and everything else in their rooms.

NF children love toys that can be personalized; they give a name and even a personality to every stuffed animal they possess. If a parent, in cleaning an NF child's room, happens to believe there are too many stuffed animals in the room and gives several away, that child will be devastated by the loss. To NF children, losing a stuffed animal is like losing a close friend.

WHAT CAPTURES THE NF CHILD'S ATTENTION

One of the central characteristics of NF children is their imagination. Toys, books, even furniture can take on incredibly imaginative meaning for them. It is usually the NF children who have imaginary playmates. NFs are very sensitive to how a parent responds to their imaginative friend or to the imaginative story they weave around a stuffed animal, a GI Joe figure, or a special doll. Parents may worry that their child is losing touch with reality when what is really happening is the natural development of a very active imagination.

So what gets NF children's attention is anything that gives them *personalized* attention. Whereas SJ children long to be appreciated so they know they are in the right place and doing the right thing, NF children want more than just appreciation. They want the appreciation personalized and individualized for them alone. "Do you really feel that way *about me?*" is the question they might ask that makes them different from SJ children. They need to be known and appreciated by others, but they want it to be specifically for themselves.

We'll see this need for relationships also develop over time in a way that is unique to NFs. They live a paradox: They want to be recognized as part of the group and to be acknowledged by others in the group, but at the same time they demand that they be treated as individuals who are autonomous from the group. As we'll see, much about NF children is paradoxical.

HOW NFs HANDLE VARIOUS SITUATIONS

School
School is important to NF children primarily because that is where their friends are. They can have strong feelings about the teachers as well, tending to idolize a teacher who will show them personal attention and warmth. They want to be loved and respected by the teacher. In many cases,

125

they will also try to take care of the emotional needs of the teacher they love. They like to give little gifts to the teacher, just to let that teacher know that he or she is loved.

On the other hand, NFs can have extremely negative feelings, often described in their own words as a passionate hatred, toward a teacher who is impersonal or who ridicules a child in the classroom. NF children have an incredible sense of fairness, and the teacher who is unfair or unfeeling and ridicules others is to be avoided at all costs. It doesn't matter if the unfairness or ridicule affects the NFs directly or not; they will take an unwavering position against such a teacher.

NF children love to talk about what they are learning, therefore group discussion—especially small-group discussion—was invented by NFs and for NFs. Being in a classroom that is arranged in rows feels very impersonal to NFs. They much prefer to sit around small tables, where they can interact easily with others. Their need to talk about what they are learning can lead them to talk to their neighbors in the class. Sometimes they are talking simply to be talking; most of the time they are verbalizing what they are internalizing about the subject being studied.

NF children, like NT children, love to read and be read to by an adult. At an early age they enjoy having books read to them that they can't yet read themselves. But what is unique to NF children is that they enjoy books that spark their imaginations. Fairy tales or other imaginative stories can be read to them over and over again. Eventually, they even feel that the main characters in their favorite stories have become their personal friends, having built a deep identification with Winnie-the-Pooh or Alice in Wonderland. For this reason, it is good for the parent to monitor what the NF child is reading.

NF children love classes that in some way touch their emotions or focus on people. Classes such as music, literature, languages, and social studies would be among their favorites. Usually they are pleasant and agreeable students who want to please the teachers they enjoy. They love the challenge of learning, so difficult or boring classes can be tolerated as long as taking those classes somehow fits in with some future goal for them. Overall, they generally do well academically, especially with the right teachers.

When NF children prepare a class project, it is often presented "from the heart." The slightest critique, even if it is done through the grading process, can be devastating to them, way out of proportion to what was intended. Critiques need to be sandwiched between warm and personal praise for the effort and quality of work that was presented. When making an oral presentation, NF children are often the ones who can "wing it" and who will frustrate the overly prepared SJ children.

The percentage of NF children in a classroom is very much the same as the percentage of NT children in a classroom. In a class of thirty-two, approximately four children would be NFs, and only one of those four would be an Introverted NF. Introverted NF children can be painfully shy and hypersensitive in the classroom, especially if the teacher is impersonal or overwhelmed by the class. NF children often report that they feel "out of step" with the other children in their class. They often feel this way until they reach college, where classes and instructional values are more oriented to the iNtuitive person.

Tasks
The best way to approach NF children about a task is to put it in the context of a relationship. If they need to clean their

room, doing it with them will help keep them motivated and active. If left alone to clean their room, Introverted NFs are likely to get lost in their imagination over some item they were putting away. Extraverted NF children will feel too alone and find a reason to keep coming to where you are—asking you numerous questions, for example.

The other important thing to remember about NF children and tasks, such as homework, chores, or cleaning their room, is that everything they do needs to have some meaning to it. If they ask why, they are not trying to understand the rationale for the task; they are trying to fit this particular task into their whole scheme of life or into their relationship with you as the parent. But sometimes even meaningfulness isn't enough; some NFs will simply not finish the task because they got lost in a daydream, which is a favorite pastime.

Their room will not be the neatest in the house, for there are other things much more important than a neat room. One NF mother said of herself that "a tidy house is the sign of a misspent life." Since reality is very subjective for NFs, they are much more interested in meaningful things than in routine things like keeping a room or a house clean. They can be very idealistic, even to the point of being perfectionistic about some things. But generally it is meaning that motivates them to do various tasks.

Family and holidays
NF children are very oriented to family and to holidays, for these are seen as the context of important relationships. They enjoy traditions that are meaningful. And since it is people who give the primary meaning to traditions, they can even forgo the tradition as long as they have the relationship. If every Thanksgiving you go to Grandma's house,

but this year Grandma is in the hospital, the tradition is quickly forgotten and replaced by the urgency to get to the hospital and talk to Grandma.

NF children are very sensitive to the feelings and moods of others. If there is parental conflict in the family, they will usually withdraw from family interaction and experience high levels of insecurity. Often their response to family conflict or to feelings of insecurity is to develop physical symptoms. I am an NF, and as a child I experienced an ulcer at age ten due to the stress in our family related to my father's temper.

The ideal family life for NFs would have its established routines but would also allow for a lot of interaction among family members. NFs can be very sensitive to a new child coming into the family, because then all the relational patterns must be reworked. They wonder if they will still be valued as people. Promises are very important to NF children and must be kept if at all possible. When promises have to be broken within a family, the reasons need to be clearly spelled out, though that may not be enough. The truth is, to NF children there never is a good reason to break a promise.

NF children can also struggle with problems with anger more than children with the other temperaments do; this is especially true for Introverted NFs. Often their expectations for themselves, as well as for others, can be so high that they end up feeling betrayed and deeply hurt. Their response is often anger that they don't even understand. They are also deeply disturbed by anger in others since, because of their sensitivity, they don't have the emotional defenses that other children may have.

Discipline

It is easy to overdiscipline NF children. Because of their sensitivity and desire to please, harsh discipline is usually completely unnecessary. Often all that is necessary is a slight raise in volume of a parent's voice. Sometimes a raised eyebrow or stern look will do to bring quick tears and repentance from NFs. Taking the time to explain the meaning behind the raised eyebrow or raised voice will usually make a strong and lasting impression on these children. Harsher forms of discipline should be reserved for those extreme situations where danger exists or where the children are actively being rebellious. Of course, any child can be rebellious, especially when overdisciplined or when the discipline seems consistently unfair. That's why it's important to understand what works best with each type of child.

Responsibility

Because of the importance of relationships in the lives of NF children, even the very young, they tend to be very responsible, especially if the parents can frame the need for responsibility around the children's relationship with friends and family members. Parents need to remember that NF children's strengths are very global and impressionistic, and therefore these children have very little awareness of the specifics or the details. This is something parents need to help NF children become aware of, but the task will be more in helping them understand their own limitations rather than in helping them learn to see the details of life. If a task is very detailed, parents may need to work alongside their NF children, for this is a genuine blind spot in this temperament.

Relationships

What NF children cannot do with detail they make up for when it comes to relationships. Friendships give NF children and adults meaning in life. The knowledge that they are valued by other people gives them a sense of identity.

Their relational abilities show themselves in that they are usually a good judge—even when they're young—of other people's character.

Competition has very little appeal to NFs. They may be playing a game and enjoying the interaction with the other kids. But when it appears that someone is going to lose, NFs may use their move to help that person out and keep them from losing. If it's Monopoly, they may lend money to the one out of money or say, "Pay me later" when he or she lands on their property. All of this upsets the other players, especially if they are not NFs! The NFs' sensitivity to other people's feelings means that if someone loses, they suffer along with the loser. NFs are much more interested in cooperation than in competition. This is true on the playground just as much as it is in the classroom. Competitive grading is meaningless; liking the teacher and the subject is what counts.

In early years, NF children may offer to give their toy to the little one who is crying because someone else won't share a toy with him. The four-year-old NF may sit there and negotiate a workable arrangement with the desired toys so that both the other kids are happy. On the other hand, if she is the recipient of a child's hostile takeover of a toy she is playing with, her tears will likely be more satisfied by a hug from the child who took the toy than by getting the toy back from that child.

SOURCES OF STRESS FOR THE NF CHILD

Because their feelings are so important, one of the major stressors in the life of NF children comes when someone wants them to justify or explain their feelings in a situation. They may be filled with feelings, but they can neither justify nor explain them anymore than the adult NF can. When your NF child is filled with indignation because of the way the teacher treated one of the children in the classroom, it is best to let your child know that you understand the intensity of what she feels and that it is OK for her to have these feelings, even if you can't understand the so-called injustice.

The other thing that can stress NF children is being forced to compete. We've already noted how this is. If they are on a school team or just on a team on the playground, talking and interacting with friends will take preference over the need to win—especially winning at all costs. Often NFs are the last to be picked, not because they don't have the ability to play the game but because they don't have that "killer" instinct that is needed to win at all costs.

Procedures can also be very stressful to NFs. Having to focus on one thing at a time can cause them to shut down. In the same way, being forced to work too much with a lot of details may stir up all kinds of internal resistance. In one sense, both of these pressures are an attempt to get iNtuitive children to use their Sensing function—something they may not be able to do very well until much later in adulthood.

Perhaps the biggest source of stress for NF children is the feeling that someone doesn't like them. If they know they have done something to offend another person, they will work to make things right with him or her, if possible. But if in doing this they still feel that the other person doesn't like them, in spite of what they have done to repair the damage, NFs may not rest until they have completely won over that other person. If this is impossible to accomplish, they will simply give up with that person and act as if he or she no longer exists.

SPECIAL PARENTING TASKS WITH AN NF CHILD

It is important for parents of NF children to understand how important friendships are to those children. If a parent is not an NF, this may be very difficult to understand. SJ or NT parents may see the NF's need for people as a crutch or as irresponsible behavior. Criticism by these parents can be devastating to NF children, particularly because of their sensitivity. This is especially true when it comes to discipline. SJ or NT parents may want to base discipline on some rational basis, such as a specific rule, or on some impersonal procedure, such as "If you . . . , then. . . ." Both of these approaches ignore the interpersonal context of the child's behavior and therefore are lost on NF children—which then negates the impact of the discipline. It's very important to listen to any child, but especially to NF children as they attempt to explain the context of their perceived misbehavior.

It takes time to understand NF children, for they have a special complexity and are often misunderstood by those of other personality types. If parents can understand the centrality and importance of relationships to their NF children and build strong relationships with those children, they have won most of the battle. Warmth and caring are the ground rules with these children; therefore, you will get much more from them this way than with harshness or coldness.

THE EXTRAVERTED NF AND THE INTROVERTED NF

When we look at the differences between Julie and Daren, the Extraverted NFs, and Jennifer and Dan, the Introverted NFs, on the playground, we again see that it is a matter of quantity. Julie and Daren enjoy multiple friends, whereas Jennifer and Dan enjoy one or two friends at a time. The Introverted NFs' small circle of friends, though, will often be friends for a lifetime. The relationship needs of Extraverted NFs may also be focused more intensely on two or three special friends, but for them, there will also be a large number of other friends who can become just as important at any given point in time.

If the friends are away, Introverted NFs may be perfectly satisfied to play alone. This would seldom be a satisfactory arrangement for the Extraverted NFs. Perhaps that is why Extraverted NFs like to keep a large number of friends around; they will never have to be alone.

IN SUMMARY
Remember, the NF child

- often lives life through her imagination
- is naturally social
- often personalizes her toys
- can attach meaning to a lot of "meaningless" things
- thrives on personalized attention
- struggles with being a part of the group yet maintaining individual uniqueness
- loves school because that's where the friends are
- hates school if there are no friends there
- wants to be loved by the teacher
- likes to talk about what she is learning
- loves to read and be read to
- responds best to tasks if they are put into the context of a relationship
- isn't too concerned with a neat room
- loves family and special days
- is very sensitive to family conflicts
- can handle routines if done in the context of interacting

- often struggles with anger because of her own high expectations
- doesn't need harsh discipline—only a raised eyebrow
- learns responsibility through interactions of relationships
- doesn't like competition—plays games in order to interact with others
- finds it hard to justify or explain her deep feelings
- needs parents to understand how important her friendships are to her

CHAPTER NINE

Helping Your Child Develop His or Her Own Way

We were talking with friends whose daughter Laurie had just learned that she was an ENFP. Both parents, as well as Laurie's three siblings, were all clearly SJs. As the parents of this young teenager were reading through the description of their daughter's personality, they kept saying things like "Oh, my" and "I can't believe it." When I asked them what surprised them the most, they said, "We just can't believe that Laurie's personality can actually be identified. We just thought she was strange."

They struggled with this child because she was so different from everyone else in her family. Everyone in the family but Laurie loved closure on things. They always finished a task as soon as possible. But Laurie never seemed to finish anything until the last minute.

Everyone in the family except Laurie approached things from a practical perspective, while Laurie was always exercising her imagination and appeared to care little about practical things. In addition, the other family members had had terrible communication problems with Laurie, because Laurie was never able to say everything she was thinking. She wasn't even aware of some things until a couple of days later. Her parents and her siblings were frustrated with her and often said to her, "But you said. . . ."

As I observed Laurie's parents' amazement over their discoveries about her, I wished I had said something to them earlier about how similar Laurie's personality was to that of my wife, Jan's. I realized again how important it is to not only understand a child's personality but to also have some frame of reference with which to compare it.

We've had a similar experience in our own family, where one of our children was quite different from the rest of the family. Since these preferences seem to be genetically determined, we wanted to see where they might have come from. Apparently, just like the color of your children's eyes, where one child's eyes are colored differently from the rest of the family's, you will find a basis for the difference in personality type by looking back a generation. If you do so, you will usually find a relative whose personality is quite similar to that of the child.

Usually each child in the family is similar to a parent or to someone else in the extended family. One of our children is different from the rest of us in that he is Judging, whereas everyone else in the family is Perceiving. We didn't know this while he was growing up. We caused him all kinds of frustration over the years. He would ask us a question, wanting a simple, definitive answer—wanting the end product. But we thought he wanted to know the process we used to arrive at that answer. Often he never got the answer because, out of frustration, he would give up and walk away saying, "All I wanted was a yes or a no."

Once we realized this, a lot of misunderstandings made sense to us. And then we took it a step further and looked throughout our extended family to see where this trait could have come from. We discovered that my mother has this trait, his maternal grandfather had this trait, and our son and his grandfather shared the same preferences in all four areas of personality. Jan's oldest brother also shares this personality profile. By having these reference points, we were better able to understand the personality of this particular child.

Understanding Your Child Better

Take some time now and look at the personality of each of your children. Whom are they like in your extended families? List below the name of each of your children and then the names of other family members who you feel share the same personality style.

YOUR CHILD'S NAME	WHOM THEY ARE MOST LIKE
_____	_____
_____	_____
_____	_____
_____	_____
_____	_____
_____	_____

WHAT HAPPENS WHEN WE DON'T UNDERSTAND

Several years ago a young woman named Gail came to me for counseling. As she described the problems she

139

wanted to work on, it sounded to me as though she was describing, in a negative way, the traits of an Introvert. Without indicating what I was thinking, I asked a number of questions, and her answers confirmed that she was indeed an Introvert. She felt that there was something wrong with her because she was this personality type. As we talked about her family, it became equally obvious that everyone else in her immediate family was an Extravert. Not only were they all Extraverts, they appeared to operate on the premise that being extraverted was the only normal way to exist in life.

The child will feel judged and unaccepted.
All during her growing-up years, the message Gail received from the members of her family was that something was wrong with her because she was different from them. She felt judged rather than accepted and affirmed. When a child's preferences for any of the eight traits differ from those of others, especially family members or a teacher or another important adult in the child's life, that child may feel abnormal and judged for being different. When these differences are not valued and respected by others, these children may feel flawed or deficient. This was exactly what Gail had been struggling with for as long as she could remember.

The child will suppress natural preferences.
The other thing that can happen when family members and other significant people do not accept a child's individual qualities is that the child will begin to suppress her natural preference and try harder to develop the opposite preference. For example, Gail had tried to develop her Extravert side, which was not her preference. But because her natural bent was introversion, the end result was that she was uncomfortable and felt inadequate with both extraversion and introversion. She hadn't developed a sense of balance;

instead, she experienced tremendous internal conflicts over the supposed wrongness of her introversion and the unnaturalness of her extraversion.

The same principle is at work with the other pairs of traits. When family, job, authority figures, or circumstances force us to suppress our natural bent and we try to act out the opposite trait, we will not find balance between the two. We will also develop internal conflict and a sense of inadequacy. We have each of these traits within us, but we prefer one over its opposite. This is like having two hands and preferring to use primarily our right or left hand. If we don't know our preference or have been told that our preference is wrong, we experience an internal conflict that can be likened to our being ambidextrous.

I talked with a friend who is ambidextrous and uses both hands to write. He explained that when he writes creatively, he has to use his left hand. But no one else can read his writing when he writes with his left hand. So when he writes a check, he has to stop and remind himself to use his right hand, and then he writes very slowly, but at least others can read what he writes. He isn't really comfortable writing with either hand.

HOW TO HELP YOUR CHILD DEVELOP HIS STRENGTHS

By now it is clear that individual differences are normal parts of our personality development. So how do parents help their child develop so that his full potential as a person created in God's image can be realized?

Don't try to strengthen a child's weak traits.

An important principle when it comes to personality is that we do *not* work directly on our weaknesses. If we encourage our child to develop his weak traits, we are creating the same conflict within the child as when we do not accept his strong traits. If we are trying to help our iNtuitive child to be more detail oriented and practical, we are basically rejecting the strengths he has as an iNtuitive child.

Encourage the child to develop his strong traits.
We help our child the most by encouraging and affirming the strengths of his personality. For example, when we encourage our iNtuitive child to develop his natural abilities as an iNtuitive, we are encouraging him to develop one of his strengths.

An interesting thing happens when we encourage the child's preferred traits and don't focus on his unpreferred traits. Over time he will become more skilled in those traits that are his preferences. This skill will cause him to feel more confident and competent in general. And that confidence and competence will give your child the freedom to begin developing the weaker personality traits as well. Thus, the iNtuitive child, when encouraged in his iNtuitive traits, will eventually develop his Sensing traits.

Remember that well balanced *has a unique meaning when applied to personality.*
As parents, our inclination will be to target what we perceive to be our child's weakness and try to get the child to work on that weakness. This is a natural response, because parents want their children to grow up well balanced. For instance, we aren't satisfied that he reads well but can't add or subtract figures; we want to see him succeed in every subject so that he will be better prepared for adult life.

When it comes to personality, however, balance is achieved not by targeting and working on weaknesses but by encouraging strengths. Personality is not merely a skill to develop—it is an intricate part of who your child is. *He must believe that who he is is OK, and he will learn to believe that through you.* When he experiences this acceptance of who he is, he will have more emotional freedom and energy to develop other traits that don't come as naturally to him.

So as parents, you will need to practice some restraint if your child's personality seems much different from your experience of "normal." Relax so your child can relax too. Find out who he is and learn to appreciate and celebrate it—and he will too. And then watch him continue to grow as a whole person!

SPECIFIC WAYS TO HELP CHILDREN DEVELOP THEIR STRENGTHS

Helping the Extraverted child

- Accept his need to talk. Interact with him and recognize that not talking can be very frustrating to him.
- When he finally gets burned out by all his interaction with others, let him sleep or at least rest. When he wakes up, he'll be talking a blue streak again.
- Encourage him to participate in team sports. So much of his fun will simply come from his being with the other kids. If he shows no interest in individual sports, don't try to push him in that direction.
- Help him see that when an Introverted friend temporarily shuts him out, it's probably because the friend needs a break, not because he (the Extravert) has done something to offend his friend.

Helping the Introverted child

- Recognize that she is drained of energy by interaction with other people. When you see her getting overly tired through interaction with friends, help her take a break and rest a bit.

- Accept her need for solitude. Her need to play alone at times does not indicate there is something wrong with her. It is her natural bent.
- Encourage individual activities such as reading, learning a musical instrument, or individual sports.
- Learn to tolerate some reluctance on her part to enter into new activities. Don't let her off the hook and allow her to not participate at all; encourage her to watch awhile and then help her participate.

Helping the Sensing child

- Learn to tolerate some dirty hands and faces. These are the result of her play, which is important to her.
- Take her to museums, especially those that allow children to touch and play with various exhibits.
- Encourage her in physical activities such as sports. Letting her take lessons in some activity that interests her can help her develop the Sensing side of her personality.
- Help her understand the practical side of some of her classes that seem irrelevant to her.

Helping the iNtuitive child

- Encourage him to read broadly.
- Take him to plays.
- When he has an imaginary friend, join in imaginative play.
- Encourage him to make up stories.
- When the iNtuitive child begins a project, get involved with him, helping him stay focused so he can finish the project.

- When he comes up with creative ways to do chores, get into the project with him, asking questions about what he is doing as he does it.

Helping the Thinking child

- Encourage the Thinking child's reasoning abilities by asking her opinions on various subjects.
- Think of her as an "efficiency expert in training"; ask her to analyze the various ways tasks are assigned and done around the house.
- When there is a procedural problem with something going on in the family, appeal to the Thinking child to help the family understand the rules and how they apply in this situation.
- Get her a computer at an early age, and give her books of puzzles to work on.

Helping the Feeling child

- Show him a lot of affirmation regarding his role in the family.
- Enjoy stories and videos of families from within our country as well as those from other countries.
- Talk about your feelings and his feelings when something happens that is disturbing to him or to you.
- Share projects with the Feeling child, making them family activities in which everyone gets involved.

Helping the Judging child

- Help her finish a task rather than urge her to "just let it go for now."
- Make certain you follow through on things you've promised to do for her.
- Help her make a distinction between what she really is

responsible for—her own things—and what she is not responsible for—other people's responsibilities. Her need to tie up loose ends can lead her to "help" other people tie up theirs—and often they don't want her help!

- If you're a Perceiving parent, help her understand the differences between Perceiving and Judging traits, and encourage her to be tolerant of the more open-ended approach to life.

Helping the Perceiving child

- Don't nag him to get things finished. Instead, work out a realistic schedule that makes sense to him, even if it seems rushed or disorganized to you.
- Help him understand that his Perceiving preference is a valid trait that has its own gifts. Help him also see that this trait can easily frustrate someone of the opposite preference, like a Judging parent.
- Encourage him to work out his own sense of order. Don't accept chaos, sloppy work, or a dirty room merely as results of his personality. He can and must develop order in his life, but that order must make sense to him.
- Accept his tendency to say yes to too many things. At the same time, help him better understand his own time limitations and learn not to overextend himself.

BE AWARE OF SHIFTS IN YOUR CHILD'S PERSONALITY DEVELOPMENT

We don't work on all four of our child's personality preferences at once. In fact, in the younger child, we will probably see only one of these four traits, or functions, being developed, since they develop sequentially at first.

Then, during the elementary school years, we may see the child working on developing one trait at any given point in time. As we notice which one is being used predominantly by a particular child, we can add to the development of that trait by encouraging it through the activities just described under each trait. As the child grows and approaches adolescence, we will often see the child depend less on that particular trait and more and more on the second trait that makes up her personality. We can then encourage the development of that trait in the same way we encouraged the development of the first trait.

For example, as Colleen moves through her early years in elementary school, we see her using her iNtuitive abilities more and more. She is developing her imagination through stories she makes up (sometimes to the dismay of her parents). As she plays with her friends, she is always changing the rules to suit some imagined idea that would make the play more fun. In her classroom she sometimes gets caught daydreaming as she lets her imagination take her out of the classroom to who knows where. She loves to read, especially stories about other people in other places. Sometimes she will "redo" the story, giving it her own twist as she reads it to her dolls or to her grandma.

But as Colleen begins to wind down her elementary-school years, she makes a shift. The Feeling part of her personality begins to show itself more and more. She reads less and spends more time on the phone with her friends. She begs her parents for a pet, even if it is only a fish. She wants something to care for and take care of. Now her problems at school are not her tendency to daydream. Instead, the teacher is concerned because she tends to talk a lot when she's not supposed to. As Colleen makes this shift in her personality development, her mom and dad need to relax and know that she is simply shifting from one strength to another in her personality, and they need to encourage both traits as she continues to develop.

What to Do about the Opposite Traits

Parents can help a child develop skills in the area opposite of her preference. These are specific abilities that a child can learn to do that are necessary for her success as an adult. *We are not working on the weakness of the personality—we are simply filling in some gaps by teaching specific skills.*

For example, parents can tell their Introverted child to "go up to the lady and tell her thank you." This is not a natural ability of the Introverted child, but she needs to learn how to do this. Parents err when they expect their Introverted child to do this naturally. It is a skill that must be patiently taught to an Introvert.

While an Extravert is generally quicker to pick up social courtesies that make for smooth relationships, in the same way, parents need to help their Extraverted child learn the skill of appreciating and using quiet and solitude. Noting times when the Extraverted child is sitting quietly, either absorbed in a book or in the stillness of a rainy evening, will help her value these moments, but they will not be sought after naturally unless they are taught.

The Sensing child will need help from parents in setting short-term goals and in placing events into a bigger picture. These are not things the Sensing child will do naturally if left to herself. Wise parents know the Sensing child will never excel in setting goals, but in order to help her develop into a successful adult, they will teach skills in goal setting as well as other skills that will help her consider the bigger picture. At the same time, the parent knows not to expect the Sensing child to do any of this naturally.

The iNtuitive child will need to be taught skills in handling the details in her life. The last thing the iNtuitive child wants to do is get bogged down in the details—and that's how it will feel to her. But parents can teach the iNtuitive child some skills related to checking the details. When the iNtuitive child prepares a class project, a wise parent will help her go through her work, checking the details. The parent may do this with the child, agreeing as they do it together how boring and tedious the whole process is. In doing so, the iNtuitive child is learning some important skills.

The Judging child will need understanding as the parents attempt to teach her skills in letting a task go before it is finished so she can experience something else. For the Judging child, flexibility is not a natural gift but a skill to be learned. When things don't go as planned, you will need to help the Judging child learn how to adjust to changes in plans and accept them as being part of life. Suggesting alternatives early in the process can be helpful. Showing the Judging child how to set up "closure points" along the way in a task, such as intermediate stages that can be considered "finished," will help her pace herself better in bigger projects.

The Perceiving child will need to be taught how to better organize her external life in a way that works for her. The organizational skills of a Judging parent will only frustrate the Perceiving child. She needs her own style of organization. She will also need help in pacing herself in class projects, especially those big reports. Help her set "mini-deadlines" for specific tasks along the way. For example, a class research project might have as one deadline a date when the research is to be finished. Another deadline might include setting a time (near the real deadline, of course) for when the outline must be finished. The Perceiving child needs to learn early that organizing big projects will always take extra effort on her part.

The common thread through each of these examples is that the parent is teaching skills to the child that the child will not develop naturally. As parents do this, they must keep in mind the fact that these skills are not to take the focus away from the *natural* development of the child's four preferences. Parents need to communicate acceptance and approval of the individual preferences of each child and then capture opportunities to teach a skill that will fill in the gap left by their child's natural type development.

A SPECIAL WORD ABOUT THE EMOTIONAL SIDE OF LIFE

All parents need to be reminded of the importance of helping their children develop the emotional side of their lives. Studies show that intellectual intelligence (the standard IQ scores we all sort of know about even though the teacher was supposed to be the only one who knew them) can only predict success in school. It cannot predict success in life. I think every parent is concerned about both. Parents want their children to succeed in school, but they are even more concerned that their children succeed in life.

Men who prefer the Thinking function are usually very unaware of their own emotional life and are unable to read much of the emotional life of others. Men who prefer the Feeling function are usually a little better at understanding their emotional life but may still be limited in their ability to read the emotions of others.

Women, in general, whether they prefer the Thinking function or the Feeling function, are much better equipped to not only read their own emotional life but to also read the emotions of other people.

The ability to read our own and others' emotions scale
There seems to be something in the way we train our female children that teaches them how to develop their emotional intelligence—i.e., their ability to read their own feelings and the feelings of others—that we don't teach our male children.

As one thinks about the different ways little boys are treated compared to how little girls are treated, we can see a number of things that limit a boy's ability to develop his emotional life. Little boys are not supposed to cry, nor are they supposed to be sensitive to other children's feelings. (We don't want him to be a sissy.) But attitudes like these serve only to limit little boys in the development of their emotional skills.

Daniel Goleman, in his study *Emotional Intelligence,* points out the three most common mistakes parents make in dealing with their children's emotions.

1. **"Ignoring feelings altogether."**[4] Parents who make this mistake fail to take advantage of teachable opportunities. Some parents ignore the feelings of both male and female children, thus limiting those children's emotional lives not only as children but just as certainly as adults. But notice how often parents will ignore the hurt feelings of a son, telling him to "suck it up and be a man." These same parents will pick up a daughter and comfort her, talking to her and listening to her hurt feelings. If parents want to help both Thinking and Feeling children grow emotionally, they need to use emotional situations involving the children as opportunities to comfort, affirm, and acknowledge

feelings as OK. This can help children learn important lessons in handling their emotions.

2. **"Being too laissez-faire."**[5] In this style, parents notice that a child is upset but do little, if anything, about it. If a child is hitting another child, the other child's parent is left to deal with it. If a child is having a tantrum or is pouting, the parent offers the child a bribe to smooth things over. These parents don't ignore emotional situations, but they don't grab hold of the teachable moments either. What they tend to do is minimize the hurt a child may be experiencing and then not check out their perception with the child to see if it is accurate. This kind of indifference will not help a child develop emotional abilities.

3. **"Being contemptuous, showing no respect for how the child feels."**[6] These parents handle a child's emotional upset with harshness and criticism. If the child is irritable, they will punish the child rather than attempt to understand what is going on with him. Often, parents who use this style will forbid a child to be angry with an adult. Any frustration in the child as he deals with a parent is met with stern disapproval and even additional punishment. Children who are not allowed to experience their own emotions can develop serious emotional problems lasting well into their adult years.

In regard to these three different parenting styles, studies show that parents tend to treat a son this way much more often than they would a daughter. As a result of these negative emotional experiences, the typical male child is going to grow up emotionally incompetent, regardless of his preference for Thinking or Feeling.

What can parents do to help shape the emotional intelligence of their child and avoid the unhelpful, even damaging, parenting styles described above? For one thing, we can look at how we raise little girls. From an early age, most little girls are given the ingredients for emotional growth. There are exceptions, but generally their feelings are valued and noticed. They may be taught to know what kinds of behaviors are expected in different situations. Little girls are taught to effectively control their emotional impulses, especially the impulse to misbehave. Little girls, much more than little boys, are taught to wait patiently for something and to delay self-gratification for the sake of others.

Little girls are also taught to follow directions and ask for help when it's needed. All we need to do is remember the jokes about how grown men will stay lost for what seems like hours because they won't ask for directions. We think this is a male trait, and perhaps it is. But it is more likely that as little boys, they were not taught by parents and other adults that it is OK to ask for help when needed; instead, they were taught that to ask for help is a sign of weakness.

Understanding Your Child Better

Here is a list of tasks that parents can do with their children to help develop the emotional intelligence of their sons and daughters. These suggestions are especially important in relating to sons.

1. **We need to help our children understand and name their own emotions.** This means that we as parents must understand our own emotions first. Then we are to help our children learn how to recognize their emotions and to know how their emotions are related to their actions. This includes teaching them how to communicate with others,

both about their own feelings and about what they see the other person experiencing emotionally.

2. We need to help our children understand the basis for making decisions. If the children are Thinking people, they need to understand that the best decision they can make will be based on thoughts, facts, and logic. If they are Feeling children, they need to understand that the best decision they can make will be based on deeply held values, a concern for others, and an intangible sense of what is right. Both Feeling children and Thinking children need to value the Feeling children's way of making decisions, even though Feeling children cannot give logical reasons for the decision. Parents need to model this acceptance by giving value to the contributions made by Feeling children in the decision-making process. Helping these children value their own subjective process in making a decision by giving credibility to their "gut feeling" that something is wrong will pay off as they learn to listen to those subjective responses. As Feeling children mature, they may need help in applying these decision-making skills to issues such as sex and drugs.

3. Children need to learn, both by example and by training, how to manage their feelings so they don't use verbal put-downs with either themselves or with others. They need to learn how to monitor their "self-talk."[7] The best way to teach this to your children is to be an example yourself. Being careful about what you say about other people teaches your children respect for others. Being careful about your self-talk—what you say about and to yourself—is also important and needs to be demonstrated to your children. How you talk to yourself, either out loud or

[7] See my book, *Self-Talk: Key to Personal Growth*, (Grand Rapids, Mich.: Revell, 1982, 1996).

in your thoughts, has a lot to do with what you experience emotionally. Negative self-talk cycles can create feelings of fear, self-doubt, and anger within us. Those feelings can be brought under control by changing these self-talk cycles.

For example, as a child says to himself, "I'm so stupid; nobody likes me," he is setting up a negative self-talk cycle that will erode his self-confidence, lead to self-doubt, and probably bring about depression if repeated over time. Instead of reprimanding a child for such negative thoughts, spend time with him trying to understand why he is saying and feeling those things. Only when we understand the sources of those cycles can we break them and help create positive self-talk cycles.

4. **We need to help our children understand the importance of taking personal responsibility for their decisions, actions, and emotional responses.** Again this is more "caught" than "taught." Our children need to see us taking personal responsibility for our actions. Parents need to show their children by example how to admit they were wrong to get angry or that they made a bad decision. This means that we can ask for our children's forgiveness when we have made a mistake. We can't expect them to learn to do something that we cannot do ourselves.

This list is a starting point of what we need to do as parents to help our children become more competent emotionally. We can begin doing these things immediately, regardless of the ages of our children. Begin at the earliest opportunity to do these things—starting with the very first time we hold that precious gift from God in our arms.

CHAPTER TEN

What to Do When Your Child's Style Drives You Crazy

Sometimes one of our children just rubs us the wrong way. We love him or her, but it is a real chore to live with the child. Not everything in a child that rubs us the wrong way can be explained by personality. Sometimes a child drives us crazy because he reminds us of someone else in our family who drove us crazy. But sometimes he drives us crazy because he is too much like us, reflecting very clearly our own weaknesses.

WHEN A CHILD REMINDS US OF SOMEONE ELSE

Earlier we had you note who each child was like in your families of origin. If you related one of your children to someone in your past with whom it was difficult for you to get along, perhaps you are confusing your feelings for these two people, making it difficult to see your child for the person he is.

I believe that when this happens—when we see things

in our child that remind us of someone in our past with whom we had difficulty—we need to deal with the issues of that past relationship. We may think we can separate the issues, but anything from our past that is unresolved is always seeking ways to express itself in our present. Freedom comes as we resolve the past issues.[8]

Sometimes a child reminds us of a parent with whom we have unresolved issues. There are also situations in which a child reminds us of an ex-spouse. Tom's personality was very much like his father's, even at the age of eight. He even sounded like his father when he talked. The divorce took place four years ago, but Tom's mom and dad are still at each other's throats whenever they have to talk.

Tom lives with his mother, Karen, and she came to see me because she was always angry with him. As you read this, it may seem very apparent to you what was going on. But to Karen, it wasn't clear at all. When I commented on how she was transferring all of her anger toward Tom's father to Tom, she was stunned. She must have sat there silently for five minutes, just letting that information sink in.

It wasn't easy for her to separate Tom from his father as she tried to deal with her anger. But what she realized was that for Tom's sake, as well as for her own, she needed to find a way out of the angry cycle she and Tom's father had set in motion long before the divorce.

Sometimes the connection is overly positive. Our child may remind us of someone we loved very dearly. Because in our memory we have idealized that person in our past, we also idealize our child. When this happens, that child

---

[8] For help on this, see my book *Forgiving our Parents, Forgiving Ourselves,* Vine Books, 1991, 1996. There is a workbook in the second edition to help you work through these issues.

can drive us crazy because of his failure to live up to the wonderful expectations we have placed on him and hidden deep inside us.

Understanding Your Child Better

1. What Karen needed to do first was identify whom Tom reminded her of. Whom does your child remind you of? Is it someone with whom you have unresolved issues?

2. Karen needed to clarify those unresolved issues she had with Tom's father. What was it that kept her in the cycle of anger? What keeps your issues unresolved—from *your* side?

3. Karen needed to state clearly—to herself—the loss she had experienced that kept fueling her anger. In Karen's case, a lot of her anger was due to the loss of her dream of an intact family. When she married, she was determined to never divorce. When her husband left her for another woman, Karen had no choice and really no say in the matter; the divorce happened. Clearly, one of the big losses she was still angry over was the loss of a complete home. She needed to grieve that loss, meaning she must not only experience her anger but also her sadness over that loss.

Have you dealt with the deep emotions that keep coming between you and your child? Often this kind of healing comes with the help of counseling from a pastor or a therapist.

4. Then Karen needed to forgive Tom's father for destroying her dream. This is a very difficult step, and it often takes a long time. Forgiving Tom's father would not mean that Karen condoned his actions or minimized the pain he had caused. Karen may never completely get over the pain her former husband caused, but she needed to forgive him for her own sake as well as for Tom's. She didn't need to

become good friends with her former spouse in order to forgive him. She may always need to be on her guard with him. But forgiveness is possible even then. Only through the process of forgiveness can she find true freedom.

Have you moved on to forgive the person who wronged you and who is so similar to your child? What step can you take in that direction now?

WHEN A CHILD FEELS CRAZY INSIDE

Sometimes a child is in trouble developmentally, and her struggle with learning how to grow and become a person isn't going well. That child may drive any parent crazy simply because she is probably driving herself crazy too. Sometimes this is the result of being different from those within the family and feeling that "something is wrong with me." You can check this out by using what you have learned in this book to affirm behaviors and attitudes in this child and see how she responds.

Mary had to do this with Angie, her twelve-year-old daughter. Gerry, Mary's husband, was gone a lot due to his work. He felt guilty about it, so when he was home, he was very lenient with the kids, especially Angie. He would often undermine Mary's attempts to deal with Angie in matters requiring discipline. As a result, when Gerry was gone, Angie would openly defy her mother. All of this was taking place just as Angie was entering puberty. The combination of her emerging hormones, the physical changes in her body, and the insecurity she was feeling with both Mom and Dad produced a bundle of mixed-up emotions inside her that, as she said, made her feel as if she were going to explode. Any parent would have had a hard time with Angie under those circumstances.

Here are the steps Mary and Gerry took.

1. They worked at identifying what might be causing Angie's behavior. They were able to see that Gerry's frequent absence from the house was very unsettling to Angie. Angie was clearly an SJ child who needed stability in her life. The recent changes with Gerry's working so much had pulled Angie's security rug from beneath her. Both parents felt that this was the major factor in Angie's unsettledness.

What might be causing your child to be a little crazy right now? Can you identify changes in the family, in the child's health, or at school? You may need to get additional clues from other people who see your child regularly.

2. Mary and Gerry took Angie out for dinner and shared their concerns about her behavior. But, quickly—before Angie could become defensive—they took responsibility for the unsettledness in the household at this point. They told Angie that they thought Dad's absence at home was making her feel unsettled.

At first Angie was on guard, but as she listened, she was able to hear them take responsibility for changes they had made in the home. They were not accusing her of being bad or at fault, so Angie was able to enter the conversation and share some of the fears she could identify.

Try to approach your child in a way that won't appear accusing or threatening. Give the child lots of freedom to be honest with you about what he or she is feeling. Don't hesitate to get help from a counselor in planning this approach.

3. Gerry did two things: (1) He was more supportive of Mary's attempts to discipline Angie, and (2) he made it a point to spend more time with both Mary and Angie. When

he was out of town, this was done over the phone. If he was working late at the office, he would call, not just Mary but also Angie. On the weekends, instead of focusing his attention on Mary, he also spent time alone with Angie. Within a couple of weeks, Angie's behavior had settled down.

Depending on what is causing your child's problem behavior, you will need to respond. It's important that your child sense a quick and genuine response from you. And talking usually isn't enough. Follow up your discussion with action that proves to your child that you are concerned and will make any changes necessary to help him or her cope.

WHEN A CHILD IS TOO MUCH LIKE US

Then there is the child who is too much like us. He drives us crazy because we see all his weaknesses, and those weaknesses remind us of our own. Or we struggle with things in our own life, and watching our child struggle with the same things takes the focus away from our own failures, and we become frustrated with the child's struggle with the same issue. It's a case of trying to get the speck out of our child's eye while we still have a log in our own eye. (See Matthew 7:1-5.) You can check on this one by talking with someone who knows both you and your child. Ask that person to help you understand how much of what bugs you about that child is also in your own personality.

You can also make a list of all the negative personality traits you think you have. Do this, thinking only of yourself. After you have made the list, go back over it and ask yourself how many of these traits you see in the child you are struggling with. We are often critical of the child who is like us because we know his weaknesses all too well.

But what we don't realize is that even though our person-alities may be similar, we are still uniquely different. Just because we have behaved a certain way because of our weaknesses doesn't mean our child will. I talked with a mother named Jane and her sixteen-year-old daughter, Jamie. Jane kept commenting on how much she and Jamie were alike; their names were even similar. Jane also kept commenting on how she knew how her daughter felt about everything since they were so much alike. Finally, Jamie blew up at her mother and said, "Just because we're similar doesn't mean you know everything about me. I can be my own person, you know!"

I hoped so, but I wasn't sure, for Jane had a real hold on Jamie's development, and it was very difficult for Jamie to be her unique self. She was torn between her love for her mother and her need to know herself better. One of the things we talked about their doing was to brainstorm together about all the things they could find that made them *different* from each other.

At the bottom line, Jane felt she wanted to protect Jamie from the mistakes she had made in her life. She also found that she was very critical of Jamie in those areas of personality where she and Jamie were alike. Jane and Jamie were both Extraverted Sensing Perceivers. As such, they both had a strong tendency toward being impulsive. That was one of the things that scared Jane. She was afraid that Jamie would do something foolish. Every time she brought up the subject, Jamie would remind her of her own impulsiveness, and they would argue in circles.

One time, in the comic strip "Sally Forth," Sally is con-fronting Hillary, her daughter. She tells Hillary that "this bedroom is a disaster. There is absolutely no excuse for it." Hillary comes up with a great excuse in the next little box as she reminds her mother, "But, Mom, this is your room."

Understanding Your Child Better

1. Take some time and list the things that drive you crazy about your child. Which are things you struggle with in your own life?

2. If this child is old enough, discuss what you have learned, both about your own personality and hers. As you discuss your personalities, talk about how we often see our own weaknesses (or we think we see them) in the other person and then are critical of that person for failing in the same areas we ourselves fail. If necessary, ask your child to forgive you for the ways in which you have been unfairly critical of her.

WHEN A CHILD IS SO DIFFERENT FROM US

Often the child who is a problem for us to get along with is one whose personality is different from ours in a dramatic way. The problem exists because we interpret his differentness in some personal way. It irritates us. I may think the Perceiving child's room is a mess, not because he is Perceiving but because he is defying me and doesn't care about my Judging needs for order. Or the SJ parent may interpret the NF child's daydreaming as a defiant act of irresponsibility aimed at the parent. It is important that we begin to understand and celebrate our individual differences within our family.

Lou didn't know how to do this. He was an iNtuitive Thinker who felt that all people should have at least three rational reasons for anything they wanted. This was one of the rules in his house: If you wanted anything, you had to give three logical, rational reasons why you wanted it. It didn't suffice that you just "wanted it." He had four kids, all of whom preferred the Feeling trait over the Thinking trait. So did his wife, Maryanne. Even though he was outnumbered, he ran a tight ship and everyone tried to follow his rule, especially since he was unbending about it.

The crisis that led to their coming to counseling was that, as the children got older, they realized that what their dad was doing was "unfair"—a strong Feeling word. When Maryanne started to quietly rebel against this rule, it didn't take as long for the kids to notice as it did for Lou to notice. But when he did, everyone was in trouble.

The problem was not that Lou felt he needed to teach his children some analytical skills; he simply felt that his way was the only way and that all people could be as logical and analytical as he was if they would try. All he wanted the kids to do was try. Maryanne was quick to point out that they had all tried, but no one was able to live up to his expectations. And they were tired of trying! What Maryanne was especially tired of was the lack of acceptance they all felt with Lou.

Lou struggled in several ways with the Feeling side of his personality. For one thing, he had grown up with a mother who was very impulsive in her spending, and late at night he had listened to his parents fighting about her spending. As a young man he concluded that his mother, who was a Feeling person, had a fatal flaw in her personality. She didn't know how to be logical and analytical. Of course, he married a Feeling woman, and then, somehow, had all Feeling kids. But rather than see the strengths of that part of their personalities, he was determined that they would all become like him.

It took quite a while for Lou to finally begin seeing the positive strengths of the Feeling trait as well as some of the weaknesses that went along with his Thinking preference. It was only when he was able to read some of the manuals for the *Myers-Briggs Type Indicator* and look at some of the technical reports related to the validity of the test that he was finally convinced.

Understanding Your Child Better

If you struggle with accepting a child whose personality is different from yours, do the following:

- Reread chapters 5–8 and make a list of the strengths of that child's particular personality preferences.
- Determine that at least once each day you will notice and verbally affirm a strength in that particular child. Check off each strength as you comment on it. When you have gone through all the strengths you have listed, go through them again—daily. As you do this consistently over the next weeks and months, you will be amazed at how your relationship with that child will change.
- Of course, if you want to avoid having problems with the other children, do the same with the list of strengths associated with each of their personalities.

I hope that as you come to better understand your own personality and the personality of each of your children, you will be able to see that most irritating behaviors can be understood as personality differences, which are "equally right, equally good, equally valuable, and equally appropriate."[9] It's our responsibility as parents—the ones who are more mature—to teach our children the importance of accepting our differences and for all of us to learn how to work together. We begin to do this by accepting the differences we see in our children and learning how to understand and affirm them in these areas. There really is little that is more important in our family life. But one thing that is more important is the subject of our next chapter.

[9] Charles and Connie Meisgeier, *A Parent's Guide to Type: Individual Differences at Home and in School,* (Palo Alto, Calif.: Consulting Psychologists Press, 1989), 9.

CHAPTER ELEVEN

Helping Your Child Develop Faith in God

One of our main concerns as parents is how we can foster and develop our children's faith in God. Personality certainly plays a part in our faith, not only in how we come to know God but also in how we relate to him through worship and prayer. As adults, our personality colors our appreciation of different forms of worship and different ways of praying.

For example, an Introvert will approach the whole area of prayer differently than an Extravert will. An iNtuitive will see different things in the nature and character of God than the Sensing person will. Feeling people pray for different things than Thinking people do. And Judging people will structure their devotional times quite differently than Perceiving people will. (These areas will be discussed specifically later in the chapter.)

If this is true of us as adults, it will also be true in the spiritual life of each our children. How well we understand how our children's personalities interact with spiritual matters will determine how effective we are in transmitting our faith to the next generation.

PERSONALITY AND BIBLE CHARACTERS

It is interesting to speculate about the personalities of people in the Bible. Paul and Luke were probably Extraverted NFs. Paul was a visionary who could see the whole world as his mission field. Luke wrote his Gospel and then wanted to place it into a bigger picture, so he wrote the book of Acts to complete the story. James and Matthew appear to have been SJs. Both of them leaned heavily on their Jewish traditions, were concerned with proper behavior, and were very practical in what they wrote. Peter and Mark are traditionally seen as SPs. Peter was impulsive, not only in what he said but also in what he did. Mark wrote the shortest Gospel, and his favorite word seemed to be *immediately.* John is usually considered an NT who was able to take ideas from Greek thought and weave them into the Jewish concepts of his own past, creating a Gospel for everyone. You may notice that you relate more to the Gospel written by the disciple whose personality is similar to yours.

Matthew	SJ
Mark	SP
Luke	NF
John	NT

PERSONALITY AND THE LORD'S SUPPER

Tradition has focused on four aspects of the Lord's Supper, or Communion/Eucharist. First, there is the coming together of the believers' community to do something—to share in the Lord's Table. This coming together in order to do something has a strong appeal to the SP personality. Apart from singing, Communion is the one time we all get to participate. There is action at the Lord's Table.

Second, there is the proclamation of the Word of God. Passages from the Gospels or from 1 Corinthians are read and proclaimed. The NT personality is drawn to the proclamation of the Word. We are called upon to think of the meaning of the Lord's Table, of the Savior's broken body and shed blood. There is great theology in the meaning of this act we share.

Third, at the center of Communion is the reality of the Cross. We meet together to commemorate the Lord's suffering and death. The strong sense of tradition that has grown around the meaning of the Cross appeals to the SJ personality. Believers everywhere share in this act, even though they worship differently and may even differ in their beliefs. But there is a chain of tradition that began in the upper room and also goes back to the Passover meal—a tradition that has continued uninterrupted for almost two thousand years. The SJ leans heavily upon this great traditional act.

And fourth, there is the meal itself. The NF is drawn to the meal—the bread and the wine—because the Lord's Supper is a symbolic representation of that great banquet we will share with the risen Savior in heaven. The NF thinks of this great and glorious future event and enters into the Lord's Supper as a symbol of his or her anticipation of that heavenly feast that will take place someday. NFs also enjoy the experience of believers gathered together at the table.

As we look at these different facets of our faith, obviously we are drawn to all of them. But there are specific Gospels and certain events that appeal more to us than to others because of our distinct personalities. In the same way, there will be certain parts of our faith that will appeal more to our child's personality than other parts. Let's look now at how we can appeal to a child's natural personality to help develop his or her faith.

HELPING THE SP CHILD DEVELOP HIS FAITH

The SP child's love of action will carry over into the development of his faith. His will be an active faith, so he needs to be involved in a children's or youth program that is offering opportunities to *do* things.

Conversion for the SP child will probably come at some event, when God touches the SP child in a special and personal way. Even though spontaneity is a very strong part of the SP personality, this personal commitment is very important to the SP child. He will often take the terms of his commitment very literally without thinking through the whole picture. Peter's words to Jesus that he would never betray his master are a picture of the intense commitment of the SP, but they are also a picture of the difficulty he has in following through on the daily details of living out his commitments.

To keep him involved when he's younger, spend time reading to him the great stories of Bible heroes. People like Stephen, Paul, or Barnabas will capture the SP's attention. So will the stories of David, Abraham, and Daniel. Stories of great missionaries who have sacrificed everything can help your child make his own faith practical and meaningful.

Camp—whether summer or winter—is an important event for the SP child. He always wants to go. And when he gets older, he not only wants to go to camp for kids his age, but he wants to counsel at the camp for younger kids.

Service opportunities that have a practical impact on

other people's lives will be attractive to the SP child or youth. Going on mission trips, helping at vacation Bible school in the inner city, attending summer church youth camp, or helping with the craft program in Sunday school are all possible ways to get an SP child involved in activities to exercise and strengthen his faith.

Use the natural world to inspire the SP child. The SP child is especially able to see God's handiwork in the world around him. Use outings to focus on God. If you are vacationing in a national park or watching a beautiful scene with the setting sun, teach him to pray spontaneously—perhaps a prayer of thanksgiving to God for his creation or a song of praise for the surrounding beauty. This will be a natural expression for the SP child.

Concentrate on here and now. Talking too much about the future events of prophecy or about the importance some aspect of faith will have in the SP's adult life is often meaningless for this child. His life verse might be: "So don't worry about tomorrow, for tomorrow will bring its own worries. Today's trouble is enough for today" (Matthew 6:34). To make God a reality in this child's life, your focus needs to be on the present. When you have a special worship moment, do something to commemorate it. Having a child draw a picture, write a thank-you note to God, or build a small memorial out of the stones on the ground are all ways to help the SP make his faith come alive.

Prayer is best if kept informal. When teaching the SP child how to pray, remember that he will probably not respond to formal types of prayer or strict prayer schedules. You may work for a lifetime to help him learn the importance of having a daily quiet time, only to face continual failure in that effort. It's far more important to help this child learn how to pray spontaneously throughout the day. Teach him to stop and pray whenever he experiences a "moment of awe" at some marvelous event or when he is afraid, happy, or sad. As parents, model this activity by stopping at these times during the day and praying spontaneously with your child: "Thank you, Lord, for the beautiful deer we saw in the woods today."

"Action" books of the Bible will be more appealing than other kinds. Bible reading for the SP child will probably focus on the Gospels and Acts more than any other passages in the New Testament. And usually Mark will be the favorite, for it focuses more on what Jesus did than on what Jesus taught. The Old Testament stories about people and the practical advice of Proverbs will be more interesting than the Psalms or the Prophets, at least until the SP youth has a grasp of what these people did or did not do that pleased God.

Worship needs to be spontaneous with lots of things happening. Because of an SP child's literal nature, symbolic events will not be as meaningful to him as the actual here-and-now events of worship. Singing together, testifying about what God is doing in a person's life, and preaching that is filled with practical suggestions about how to live the Christian life this week are what will help the SP child (and adult) grow in his faith.

Helping Your SP Child Grow Spiritually

Remember that

- growth in faith comes through action. He will prefer action books and action stories from the Bible.
- he takes commitments very seriously.

- he will always be fighting impulsivity.
- too much emphasis on prophecy can be depressing and scary for him.
- he needs to make something to commemorate special commitment times.
- his theme verse is Matthew 6:34.

Therefore, you can help him grow by

- making sure his faith has active outlets—mission trips, camps, and volunteer work—and that worship time for him is active.
- helping him work out the specifics of his faith commitment.
- teaching him to worship or pray anywhere and anytime.
- focusing on the heroes of the Bible and on "action" mission figures.
- exploring things he can do to commemorate special spiritual times in his life.

HELPING THE SJ CHILD DEVELOP HER FAITH

The SJ child's natural love of traditions and desire to be a responsible part of that tradition will carry over into her relationship with God. The holy holidays such as Christmas, Palm Sunday, Good Friday, Easter, and Pentecost are great opportunities for parents to help the SJ child develop her faith in the God of these holidays.

Conversion for the SJ child will probably be at her mother's knee. She wants to follow in her parents' faith. Commitment is a very serious thing for the SJ child. Whereas the SP child will make a commitment because he has been challenged to *do* something for God, the SJ child will often make a commitment because she wants to *be part of* the family of God. Like the SP child, she will also take very literally the expectations of her commitment, but the SJ child will begin to structure an organized spiritual life that will govern her relationship to God for a lifetime.

Holidays are more meaningful if they are centered around their spiritual meaning. Parents need to guard against allowing popular culture to taint important holidays for the SJ child. She will enjoy celebrating Christmas with all the normal traditions and festivities, but be sure to centralize your celebration around the birth of Jesus. This is a wonderful time to teach her about Jesus.

The Jewish festivals and holy days described in the Old Testament were great teaching events for Jewish families—and still are for many. If you have observed a Jewish celebration of Passover, you noticed that throughout the celebration the children ask, "Why are we doing this?" or "Why are we eating this?" This can be a model for the Christian parent to develop a tradition around the celebration of Christmas, Good Friday, Easter, and even Pentecost, when each year the children could ask a series of why questions, and the parents or the older children could answer them. The questions should be the same each year, with the only variation being who asks the questions.

Celebrations such as these, especially if they have some degree of continuity with the past, are important to the SJ child. She wants not only to see the connection she has to God through her faith, but she also wants to understand how her faith is connected to those who came before her. The SJ child's life verse could be Hebrews 13:8: "Jesus Christ is the same yesterday, today, and forever." Because she loves tradition, she longs for a historical faith.

The SJ child likes an agenda. She finds it easy to have devotions every day at a set time. If she has to miss, she will usually feel guilty and uncomfortable until she can get back into her established routine. One-year Bibles were created for the SJ youth, who will love the structured way to read the Bible through in a year. Bible study workbooks or other structured ways to approach Bible study will help the SJ child follow through with her intentions. She likes to know what God expects of her so she can set about doing it.

The younger SJ child will love to experience the Bible by acting out its stories. Family evenings that allow for the family members to act out a scene from the Bible followed by discussion where the SJ child can talk about it are an excellent way to help her experience the Bible, even before she is able to read it.

Structure will be helpful when teaching the SJ child about prayer. Showing a child how she can keep a prayer diary will have meaning to her. Also, giving her an outline showing her how to pray is beneficial for this type of child. For example, you might use the letters ACTS to teach her to begin prayer with **A** doration—praising and adoring God; then **C** onfession—acknowledging my sinfulness and need for forgiveness; next, **T** hanksgiving—thanking God for what he has done and is doing in my life and in my family; and finally, **S** upplication—praying for others. Creating sheets of paper with these four words or letters on them for her prayer diary will likely be appreciated and used by the SJ child.

Worship for the SJ child needs to be familiar. If major changes are made in the way the youth group or the church family worship together, the SJ child is going to struggle with those changes. She likes the prayer to come at the predictable time in worship and for the special music to be during the offering as is customary. Preaching and teaching that balance theory/theology with practical application are important for the spiritual growth of the SJ child. A model of preaching or teaching that appeals to the SJ can be seen in the book of James or in the Gospel of Matthew. The teaching is tied to the traditions of the past and pointedly looks at the implications for today.

Helping Your SJ Child Grow Spiritually

Remember that

- she loves traditions and holidays.
- she is usually converted at her mother's knee.
- she takes commitment very seriously and literally.
- she is good at activities that are structured.
- too much emphasis on prophecy can be depressing and scary for her.
- prayer needs to be practical and have a plan.
- she doesn't like change in worship.
- her theme verse could be Hebrews 13:8.

Therefore, you can help her grow by

- using holy holidays as teaching times.
- taking her childhood devotion seriously and not hesitating to lead her in a prayer of faith and dedication as soon as she shows an interest.
- teaching and encouraging her to structure her own devotional activities and commitments.
- providing her with Bible workbooks, structured devotional helps, a one-year Bible, and other reading plans.

- encouraging and helping her to act out Bible stories.
- using a tool like the ACTS prayer outline and teaching her to keep a prayer diary.
- being sensitive to her discomfort when worship services or church programs incorporate changes. You may not be able to keep the change from happening (it may be a necessary change), but you can walk your SJ child through the adjustment, respecting her feelings and helping her find new structure.

HELPING THE NT CHILD DEVELOP HIS FAITH

The NT child's natural thirst for knowledge makes him more interested in concepts and principles than in practical applications for living today. Not that the NT child isn't interested in the practical side of his faith; he assumes that he will become more competent in the practical aspects of faith if he can understand the truths and principles behind those aspects.

Conversion may come later for the NT child than for the other personality types. This is because NTs must understand things thoroughly. All their decisions (certainly major life decisions) are made after careful consideration and processing. Therefore, conversion won't be a sudden event as much as it will be a growing process over time that finally leads to a definite commitment.

He always has the overlying theme in mind. One can understand the NT child's search for faith by looking closely at the Gospel of John. John hits only the highlights of Jesus' life, but each highlight has significance. John's Gospel won't bog down the NT child with details and will thus hold the child's interest. John also focuses on the power of God as shown in the important miracles of Jesus. These are the two important approaches of the NT child in both finding and developing faith. He will be interested in the teachings of Jesus, and he will also be focusing on the power of God in the world, not only during Jesus' time on Earth but operating in the world right now.

He will always be asking why questions. The questions the NT child asks may cause a parent to worry about the strength of the child's commitment to the Lord. But when an NT child makes a commitment, it is established. The fact that he asks the why questions about the faith does not mean his commitment is wavering. He will always ask why questions; that's just part of his personality. In fact, one of the big turnoffs to the NT child is an environment that does not allow questions or that sees questions about the faith as dangerous.

Parents need to take these why questions seriously. When parents can't answer, they need to be honest with their NT child and simply say, "I don't know." If it is an important question, don't be afraid to set up an appointment with your pastor—and encourage the pastor to take the question seriously. If an adult doesn't take an NT child's question seriously, is evasive in answering, or gives simplistic answers, the NT child will have a problem respecting that adult—pastor or not—and what he or she stands for. The NT child is much like the twelve-year-old Jesus, who spent three days "sitting among the religious teachers, discussing deep questions with them" (Luke 2:46). The NT child is always searching.

He needs help setting goals and being consistent. When it comes to prayer and Bible study, helping the NT child set some personal goals for what he wants to accomplish by a set date will help motivate him to be consistent.

Some NT children will find it easy to have a devotional time every day, though the time may vary. Other NT children will be more random in their devotional times. But what will work for both types of NT children is to help them set some goals.

His approach to prayer is somewhat contemplative. Prayer can be taught to the NT in much the same way it can be taught to the SJ child. But the way the NT child prays will be different. He will often spend more time concentrating on each part of the prayer. He will pray with concepts and principles as a backdrop. He will, at times, even want to hold God accountable for what God is supposed to be doing, according to what the child has been reading in his Bible study.

Bible study for the NT child is a search for truth. At an early age he will be fascinated by inductive forms of Bible study. He will want to approach events and other passages in the Bible with the questions of a reporter: who? what? where? when? why? how? and with what?

Worship for the NT must be meaningful. It can't be done simply because that's the way it's always been done, and it can't be done simply because others like it that way. It must be done right, and the right way to do it will be centered around the written Word of God. The NT child likes songs that are based on Scripture. He likes Scripture to be read between the songs. Teaching and preaching need to be well thought out and to the point. As he enters the junior high stage, the NT child will probably know which youth leader really knows what he or she is talking about and which one is just fun and games. As in other areas of life, he will be very serious about his faith; the fun and games will not be a central part of his involvement in the youth group.

Helping Your NT Child Grow Spiritually

Remember that

- he has a thirst for knowledge.
- he likes principles and concepts more than facts.
- he is always asking questions.
- he develops his spiritual life by setting goals.
- he likes to pray about what he's read in the Bible.
- his worship must be meaningful for him.
- his theme verse could be Luke 2:46.

Therefore, you can help him grow by

- providing him study resources such as inductive Bible study guides for his spiritual learning.
- refraining from focusing on facts and details in spiritual training.
- taking his questions seriously.
- helping him set spiritual goals.
- helping him glean principles from the Bible on which to base his prayers.
- assisting him in finding meaning in worship, talking with worship leaders, if necessary, to possibly accommodate the needs of not only your NT child, but other NT children and adults in the congregation. This could be as simple as inserting more Scripture into the service.

HELPING THE NF CHILD DEVELOP HER FAITH

The NF child's natural abilities to relate to others will carry over into the area of faith. In addition, the NF's need to grow and to always have goals beyond the goals she now has will give her an open heart for a great and deep faith.

Conversion for the NF child is also often at a young
age and frequently takes place at mother's or father's
knee or with a special Sunday school teacher. But her
striving for authentic experiences (again, this sense of constantly "becoming") will often mean that the NF child will
make several commitments as she grows up. Each new
commitment will supersede the former commitment
because "now I really understand!" Wise parents will not
let their own theology get in the way of affirming these
"landmarks of growth" in the spiritual development of
their NF child. Like Paul, the NF longs to "know Christ
and experience the mighty power that raised him from the
dead." She wants to identify with and "learn what it means
to suffer with him, sharing in his death" (Philippians 3:10).
Later in that chapter, Paul adds these NF thoughts: "I don't
mean to say that I have already achieved these things or
that I have already reached perfection! But I keep working
toward that day when I will finally be all that Christ Jesus
saved me for and wants me to be" (Philippians 3:12).

Friendships are very important. The NF child is often
drawn to God through relationships. But she can also be
drawn away from God through relationships. For this reason, it is very important that she cultivate friendships with
people who can walk in faith with her. She needs to have
friends in church who are also friends in school. The consistency of friends between these two areas of the child's
life will strengthen her own commitment to the Lord. It
isn't that commitment in the NF child is weak, but her
strong commitment to other people will always compete
with her commitment to God.

**As in school, the NF child will have a favorite teacher
in Sunday school.** As the child grows older, she will gravitate toward a particular youth leader whom she respects.

She likes her heroes, both in the Bible and in the church. When one of her contemporary heroes fails, the NF child can be devastated.

One of the interesting ways to help your NF child develop her own faith is to work with her in transposing various sections of Scripture into a contemporary setting. For example, once you have read a portion of one of the Gospels, ask the NF child how that event might be different if Jesus were to repeat that scene today. You could do this with one of Jesus' parables, an event in his life as reported in one of the Gospels, or even an event from the Old Testament. The NF child will love to study the Bible if part of the study involves going beyond the study of what happened to consider what might happen if it were repeated today (remember, NFs like the test question "How else might the story have ended?").

Personalizing prayer is quite effective. One way to teach an older NF child about the richness of prayer is to suggest that she study some of the prayers in the Bible and then, after she's studied them, rewrite them as personal prayers of her own. Prayer for the NF is going to be very personal and very relational. She will pray for others fervently, beginning with the family and then extending to anyone else she knows who is in need of prayer.

She is very tuned in to spiritual realities. Of all the personality types, the NF child is perhaps the most open to the realities of the spiritual world. She takes very seriously the reality of the devil, the closeness of angels who are at work protecting us, and the realities of spiritual warfare. The younger child needs to be reminded that we are victors in this arena because of Christ's work on the cross. Symbols help the NF child internalize these powerful truths. Wearing a cross will remind the NF child of Christ's victory for her that was accomplished on the cross. Having a special place to pray and read the Bible can also be very meaningful to the NF child.

She may develop a very consistent devotional time, or she may approach it much more spontaneously. Encouraging the NF child to be consistent but allowing her to develop her own way to do it is important in helping her learn discipline. Many times she will be more consistent if she is sharing the process with a friend.

Worship times can be very powerful for the NF child. As she sings praise songs with others, she is personalizing the larger congregation's worship within herself. "What is God saying to me?" is an important question for the NF child. She will like teaching and preaching that are personal, where the speaker is able to share from experience what God is doing. Since the NF child is a good judge of character, even at an early age she can detect a phony. Because of her ability to see beyond the surface, she may get distracted from her faith by what she sees in others. She will sometimes need to be reminded that God is able to use even the phony to accomplish his purposes in our life.

Helping Your NF Child Grow Spiritually

Remember that

- her faith grows through relationships.
- she'll likely become a Christian at an early age.
- she'll often make many commitments as she grows older.
- prayer is very personal and relational to her.
- she likes to bring Scripture into the present.
- she is very aware of the spiritual world.
- she likes symbols of the faith.

- she tends to idealize favorite teachers and leaders.
- she personalizes worship.
- her theme verses could be Philippians 3:10-12.

Therefore, you can help her grow by

- encouraging friendships within the faith and attending a church that her school friends attend.
- taking seriously her early commitment and encouraging Sunday school teachers and other adults in the faith to guide her as far as she wants to go.
- respecting her need to make new commitments since this is all part of her "becoming" process.
- teaching her how to personalize prayers from the Bible.
- teaching her how to apply Scripture to here and now.
- providing her with knowledge and assurance about Christ's victory over Satan.
- providing her with symbols of her faith—jewelry, pictures for her rooms, etc.
- helping her deal with disappointment when people let her down—and reminding her of God's constancy, even when God's people fail.
- helping her discover ways to make worship meaningful to her today.

A FINAL WORD

Of course, all that we say about personality and spiritual growth is written from the human perspective. After all, that's where we are involved. The suggestions are what we can do as parents to both better understand our children's faith journey and help them as they progress along that journey.

Many times a young person walks away from his or her

faith because a parent or a church is not sensitive to the personality preferences of that child. Parents want their children to think and believe and act as they do. Perhaps a church doesn't tolerate questions, or it sees questions as wrong. Parents insist on attending a church where none of the children or young people go to the same school their child attends. These are among the issues that can become roadblocks in the development of a child's walk with the Lord.

But it is also true that both our and our children's walks with the Lord transcend the human situation. As Paul wrote to the Philippians, it is God who "is working in you, giving you the desire to obey him and the power to do what pleases him" (Philippians 2:13). Once our children choose to follow Jesus, their decision leads them into the spiritual dimension, where we as parents can only pray, encourage others to pray, and know that God is faithful to finish what he begins. God is the one who awakens our children's hearts. We want to be faithful, not only to do what we can to bring about and develop our children's faith but then to trust God to do what we cannot do.

When we have done all we can humanly do as parents and when we have ultimately turned our children over to God's power, love, and grace, there is really only one thing left for us to do: Enjoy our children as the special gifts they are!

—

CHAPTER TWELVE

Questions Parents Ask about Children, Parenting, and Personality

As we've talked with parents about their children's personalities, we have been asked many questions. We have included here some of the more frequently asked questions. As we answer these questions, perhaps we'll be answering your question(s) as well.

1. My children have very different personalities. How can I teach or at least encourage them to appreciate each other instead of calling each other "weird" or being frustrated with each other?

Children within a family are often very different from each other in personality. We have three children and four grandchildren, and they are all different from each other in one trait or another. I believe the key is for the parents to understand each child's personality. As the parents affirm and encourage each child accordingly, their acceptance of the uniqueness of each child can gradually be transferred to the siblings.

Children are more free to accept one another when they themselves feel accepted. So the more each of your children feels affirmed by you, the parents, the more free each will be to transfer that acceptance to other members of the family. Ultimately, your children will take their cues from you.

Sometimes it's helpful to plan a family discussion in which you talk specifically about the differences—as well as the similarities—you see in each other. I suggest this be a fun, lighthearted discussion, preferably not one that has been precipitated by a recent conflict.

Parents can more frequently point out a child's traits in informal comments during the course of normal activities. A Thinking child who is frustrated at his Feeling sister's failure to always be logical may need to be reminded, "You know, Denise does things for reasons, too; they're just different from your reasons. She has a gift for understanding people and being sensitive to them, and she will always see people as more important than things or ideas like you do. Don't try to argue with her when she doesn't want to argue."

An Extraverted son who keeps bothering or berating his Introverted brother may need to be reminded, "Tony helps himself rest and feel better by being off to himself for a while. That's just the way he recharges his batteries. We need to let him do that." This kind of explanation need not lead to a full discourse on personality typology, but it can go a long way in helping others in the family learn that people operate differently, and that that is all right.

It is normal for children living in the same house to pick at each other. But if the name-calling and the frustration levels become intolerable to the parents or to a child, *projection* may be the culprit. This defense mechanism is a process in which we take what we are struggling with, and, like a movie projector, we project it onto another person and then criticize that person for it. As we listen to a child pick on another child, in many cases we can learn something important about the child who's doing the picking. For example, one child has been disciplined for some misbehavior and is not feeling very good about himself. But his reaction to his bad feelings about himself is to pick on his sister and call her names. That's projection.

Much name-calling during childhood, however, is just that and not the result of projection. Sometimes a child picks on a sibling out of fun. There is a playfulness to his voice and his actions. This is not projection—he is simply being playful, even though it may greatly annoy the sibling or the parents. Listening to how your child calls someone names may help you understand how much of the conflict is a reflection of the insecurity or moodiness of the child doing the name-calling. Let's listen to this same child again, but now he has an edge to his voice and is acting sullen and withdrawn. In this mood, his picking on a sibling will simply be a reflection of his own struggle with himself. When you think insecurity or moodiness is the cause of the misbehavior, talk with that child about how he feels about himself. Also use this time to affirm the strengths you see in him.

2. How can I help my child relax a little? He's detail-oriented and very bound by duty, and I'm afraid he'll never learn to have any fun.

I would guess that your child is a Judging child, and more than likely a Sensing/Judging (SJ) child. This may sound like too simple an answer, but the first step in helping your child relax is for *you* to relax. With an SJ child this is especially important, for many times an SJ child will pick up the irritation or tension he senses in the parent and misinterpret it as judgment on what he does. And then he will simply try harder to do everything perfectly, which is the kind of overconcern you want to avoid. When the SJ child feels unaccepted, he will become more intense, more detail-oriented, and more duty-bound.

On the other hand, showing acceptance of this type of child helps to get the child talking about what he is experiencing. What is the source of his tension? Is it a teacher? a parent? peers? self-judgment? Generally you won't get this information by asking direct questions. Try to get him involved in a conversation with you. If you listen carefully, you will begin to pick up on what is stressful to him.

It sometimes helps to interject fun projects or events into the SJ child's day. You won't change his being detail-oriented. You won't change his tendancy to turn even fun things into tasks, but you can teach him to balance his time between work, play, and leisure.

3. How does puberty affect personality?

If you're the parents of an adolescent, you're probably convinced that during this period of time, personality changes drastically or disappears altogether. While this may be how parents perceive their adolescent, the truth is, adolescence is an important time in the growth of the individual personality. Much of the personality that was there during late childhood will still be there when a child leaves adolescence behind for adulthood.

During the adolescent phase of a child's development, her primary task is to establish her identity. Just as she struggled with certain developmental tasks during early childhood (using language, for instance), during adolescence she struggles with how to be a separate and unique individual yet remain connected to those she loves. "Who am I, really?" is the question the adolescent is asking when she experiments with all kinds of faddish styles. It helps parents survive these years if they have a good understanding of the child's basic personality before she enters puberty, for they will want to continue to affirm those basic traits through this sometimes stormy developmental period.

As parents affirm a budding adolescent Introvert, for example, one of the important things that particular child needs to have affirmed is that it's okay *not* be an Extravert. (This is especially true in American culture, where most people are Extraverts, and those traits are perceived to be more valuable than those of Introverts.) Pressures to experiment with being an Extravert may prove to be disastrous for an Introvert unless wise parents can affirm the strengths of that child's introversion.

One interesting development that often baffles parents during a child's adolescence is that the Judging child, who has always kept her room so neat, suddenly seems to become the Perceiving child who creates chaos in her room. Don't evaluate her personality based on how she keeps her room during these teen years. Often an adolescent's room is a safe way to rebel against the parents (which is normal) and is not an indicator of a changed personality.

4. Because of my own personality, I have more affinity for one of my children than for the other. How can I love them equally?

This is quite common, and sometimes the child we feel closest to is quite different from us. It is the child with the similar personality that may be more difficult for us to relate to, for we see all our own faults in that child.

You will feel more affinity with each child when you understand how that child operates and accept the child's traits. Often we are irritated at a fundamental level because we feel that a certain approach to life is simply wrong. Does your little Extravert drive you crazy with her chattering? Do you, the Introvert, truly think that most conversation in the world has no purpose? Yet if you see that "chattering" is your child's way of learning about the world, recharging her own emotional batteries, and processing her own thoughts, that layer of judgment you carry for "useless" conversation may fall away, at least from your relationship to that child.

Accept that you will enjoy different aspects of different children. You cannot feel "equally" about any two persons. You will like your children for different reasons. One may soothe you with her caring interpersonal touch, while the other may make you laugh at least ten times a day.

As you understand how each of your children operates, it might help to plan separate activities with each child that will help you enjoy even more that child's areas of strength or expertise. Play games with one—but do library research with the other. You'll find that each child contains rich treasures you can only begin to find and enjoy in the few years he or she is in your care.

5. How can I discipline my children according to their different personalities without appearing to be inconsistent or unfair?

As you noticed reading through the chapters on the four different temperaments, certain kinds of discipline work better with certain personalities. Parents need to be concerned with being fair, at least to a point. *But it's more important that parental discipline be effective.* A parent may decide to use time-outs with all the children, but sending an Introvert to his room for punishment may be giving him a minivacation. What appears to be fair turns out, in reality, to be very unfair.

It will help children to know that you have made deliberate choices about discipline for each of them. Talk with each of the children about how you will discipline them when they misbehave and how it may differ from how you will discipline a sibling. Listen to their concerns and discuss various options with each child. Then follow through *consistently* with what is effective with each child.

6. What do I do if my children's needs collide? For instance, my ESFJ child could spend an entire vacation at an amusement park, while the INTP child prefers to sit on the beach and read a book. One likes background noise; the other hates it. We don't want to leave either one out of a trip or vacation, but we don't have the time or money to accommodate both their preferences. Help!

This is an important question, for it allows me to underscore again that understanding our children's personalities does not mean we cater to what they like all of the time. A big part of growing up—of becoming mature adults— is learning how to compromise and to accommodate the other people in the family. Your family vacation may not accommodate either child, or it may be enjoyable to one child and just bearable to the other. Over time, you will probably provide special vacations that give satisfaction to each of your children.

Compromise is an important key. For example, you might plan a vacation that appeals more to your ESFJ child, when you hit the amusement park a couple of days and then find several other attractions to visit. During that time, you might also find a bookstore for your INTP to spend a couple of hours visiting, or there might be a museum where your family could spend a day. The ESFJ might appear to be bored at first, but the experience will probably stretch each child to learn to experience new things.

The point is that siblings need to learn to appreciate and understand each other's personality and to learn to do things as a family that may not always appeal to them. After all, isn't that the way life really is for us as adults? We don't always get to do what we want when we want to. Children can learn that things may not suit them right now but that their turn will come.

7. *This personality theory is rather new to me, so my question may sound foolish. Do I have to become three different parents if I have three kids with different personalities? How do I take care of myself while adjusting to the way each of them operates?*

Most of us as parents have already learned how to adjust in some areas to the differences between our children. We learn by trial and error that unless we are specific and concrete with one child, he will not do what we ask, whereas with another child, we learn that all we have to do is give her a look with a raised eyebrow and she will respond.

One of the values of understanding each child's personality is that it will validate some of the different ways we are already treating our children. But a more significant value is that we can also identify why certain things we do are not working with a particular child. The point is not to become three different types of parents but to understand the individual needs of each child and then better understand what is effective in relating to each of them.

You will best take care of yourself by exercising your own

good traits—as a parent as well as a person. Your children will naturally learn to adjust to you, too. And they can learn from you how to be sensitive and responsive to different types of people.

8. My child is turning out so differently from the vision I had for him when he was small. I know I need to let him develop into his own person, but I'm having a hard time with this for some reason. What can I do to get past this?

Sometimes this can be very painful. We watch a child grow and develop and then start to make poor choices that have a devastating impact on what will happen to him as an adult. The values we hold as a family, such as education, are wasted. Instead, he invests his time and energy in a pursuit that will take him nowhere. Many times, all you can do is pray, trust that God will someday get ahold of his heart again, and grieve over the lost dream you had for this child.

Sometimes our disappointments aren't so grievous. Our children grow up and are successful—they just didn't follow the path we hoped they would. In cases like these, where we have a difficult time adjusting our vision for a child who is succeeding in his own way, we usually have a personal stake in what we envisioned for that child. We want him to become something we were not able to become, and we want him to do it for our sake. That may be difficult to articulate or even to identify with, but usually that is at the root of the issue you describe. Spend some time thinking through how this may apply to you.

9. My husband doesn't buy any of this personality preferences stuff. I'm afraid he's causing a lot of turmoil to our little Dreamer. He insists on a lot of structure and rules, makes her interact and compete with kids when she doesn't want to, and is harsh in his punishments when I don't see that it's necessary. Yet I want us to appear united as parents on issues of rules and discipline. This is tearing me apart. He's not what anyone would call abusive, but I fear for my extrasensitive daughter.

Obviously, you need to begin to deal with this issue directly with your husband, and the best time is not when there has been a recent problem. In other words, choose a time when things are going smoothly to talk about your concerns. Then encourage your husband to at least read the parts in this book that describe your "little Dreamer" as well as the parts that describe his personality. Pray that God will give him an open heart to see what he needs to see.

One important thing to understand about people who don't "buy any of this personality stuff" is that their resistance is often motivated by fear. That's why your continuing insistence to get him to see the other side only causes him to dig his heels in deeper and resist more. If you can understand that his behavior is motivated by fear, you will probably be more patient with him and approach him differently than if you only see him as being resistant.

When a husband (or wife) like this refuses to budge, helping your child understand Dad's personality may be the only option open to you. After all, your Dreamer will probably end up working for a boss like Dad or even marrying someone with his traits. In this way, you can take something you see as a negative and make it a positive learning experience for your daughter.

10. How can you tell when a child is taking advantage of you, being unethical, or showing defiance rather than simply demonstrating a personality preference? I have a ten-year-old who's getting a lot of mileage out of Mom's new tolerance for his uniqueness. He argues, "That's just the way I am!" Are there times when other things must override "just the way I am"?

The answer to your last question is a resounding YES! There are, and there always will be, times when other things must override "just the way I am." My wife and I talk to many couples about their individual traits and how those traits affect the marriage relationship. When we hear of couples who use this defense, we cringe inside. The intent of understanding our own and another's personality is *never* to defend or excuse our behavior.

The purpose behind the study of personality is understanding. That means I am as interested in understanding your special personality traits as I hope you are in understanding mine. As adults, the best response is to say, "I know that's the way you are, and this is the way I am. But this situation is unacceptable. We need to find an alternative that will satisfy us both."

The same is true with children. When they use this defense—and using such a defense is actually a form of misbehavior—we deal with them the same way. We might say, "Yes, I know you're that way. But this behavior is unacceptable." And then you deal with it as you would with any other form of misbehavior.

11. Do school counseling and testing offices ever administer these personality tests? Are educators paying much attention to the personalities you've described in this book—or is school still pretty much an "SJ" world?

There are school districts scattered across the country that are training their teachers in a better understanding of children's personalities and how personalities affect learning styles. Schools are still "SJ" institutions, but some of them are trying to become more aware of the personality differences in children. I've included several books related to learning styles in the bibliography. There is also research being done in schools of education regarding the application of the *Myers-Briggs Type Indicator* in schools. If you are interested, talk with your child's principal.

BIBLIOGRAPHY

Farris, D. *Type Tales.* Palo Alto, Calif.: Consulting Psychologists Press, 1990.

Faucett, Robert, and Carol Ann Faucett. *Personality and Spiritual Freedom: Growing in the Christian Life through Understanding Personality Type and the Myers-Briggs Type Indicator.* New York: Doubleday Image, 1987.

Keirsey, David, and Marilyn Bates. *Please Understand Me.* Del Mar, Calif.: Prometheus Nemesis Books, 1978.

Kroger, Otto, and Janet Theusen. *Type Talk.* New York: Delacorte Press, 1988.

Lawrence, Gordon. *People Types and Tiger Stripes: A Practical Guide to Learning Styles.* Gainesville, Fla.: Center for Applications of Psychological Type, Inc., 1979.

Murphy, Elizabeth. *The Developing Child.* Palo Alto, Calif.: Consulting Psychologists Press, 1992.

Myers, Isabel B., and Peter B. Myers. *Gifts Differing.* Palo Alto, Calif.: Consulting Psychologists Press, 1990.

Neff, LaVonne. *One of a Kind.* Portland, Oreg.: Multnomah Press, 1988.

Wickes, Francis G. *The Inner World of Childhood.* Englewood Cliffs, N.J.: Prentice Hall, 1966.

Wirths, Claudine G., and Mary Bowman-Kruhm. *Are You My Type?* Palo Alto, Calif.: Consulting Psychologists Press, 1992.